T0064882

CONNECT & COLOR

MANDALAS

Copyright © 2016 by Racehorse Publishing

All rights reserved. No part of this book may be reproduced in any manner without the express written consent of the publisher, except in the case of brief excerpts in critical reviews or articles. All inquiries should be addressed to Racehorse Publishing, 307 West 36th Street, 11th Floor, New York, NY 10018.

Racehorse Publishing books may be purchased in bulk at special discounts for sales promotion, corporate gifts, fund-raising, or educational purposes. Special editions can also be created to specifications. For details, contact the Special Sales Department, Skyhorse Publishing, 307 West 36th Street, 11th Floor, New York, NY 10018 or info@skyhorsepublishing.com.

Racehorse Publishing™ is a pending trademark of Skyhorse Publishing, Inc.®, a Delaware corporation.

Visit our website at www.skyhorsepublishing.com.

10 9 8 7 6 5 4 3 2 1

Spot illustrations by Mary and Javier Agredo
Mandala art by Sayaka Oeno and Alexander T. Lee
Produced by Hourglass Press llc.

Print ISBN: 978-1-944686-77-2

Printed in the United States of America

CONNECT & COLOR

MANDALAS

An Intricate Coloring and Dot-to-Dot Book

Racehorse Publishing

DOT-TO-DOT GUIDE

○ = Starting Dot

◆ = Last Dot

◈ = Starting/End Dot

● = Overlapping

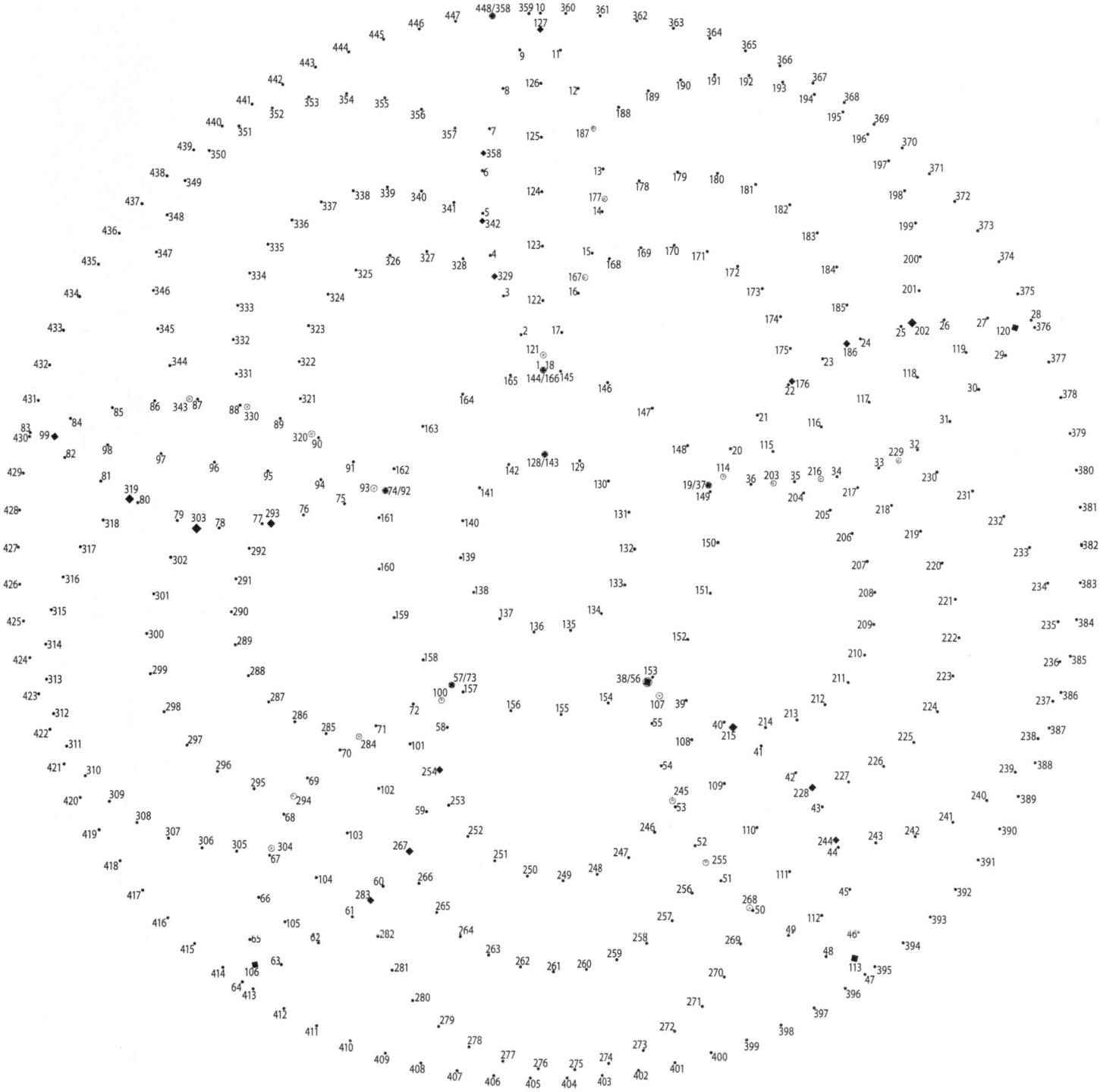

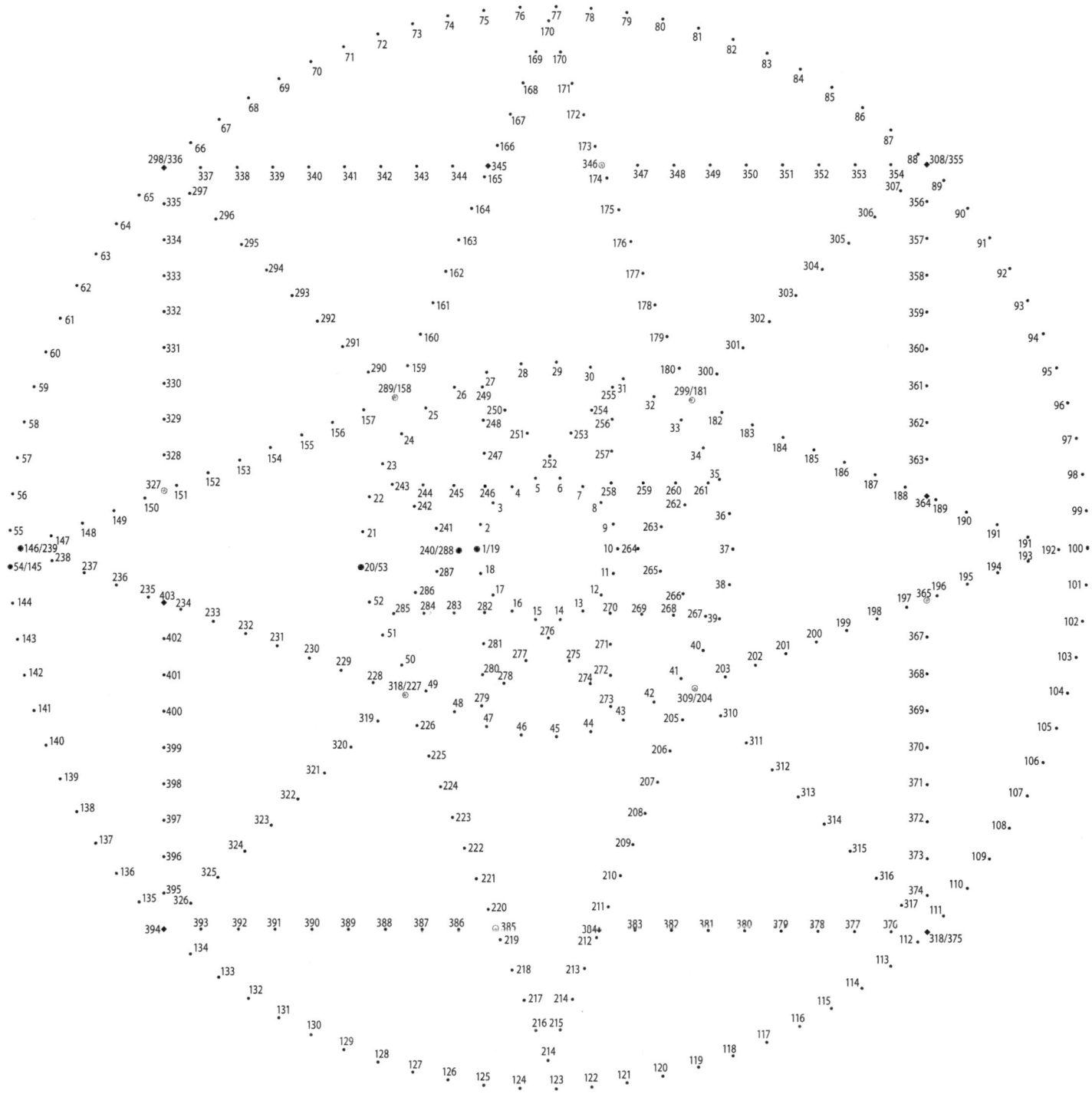

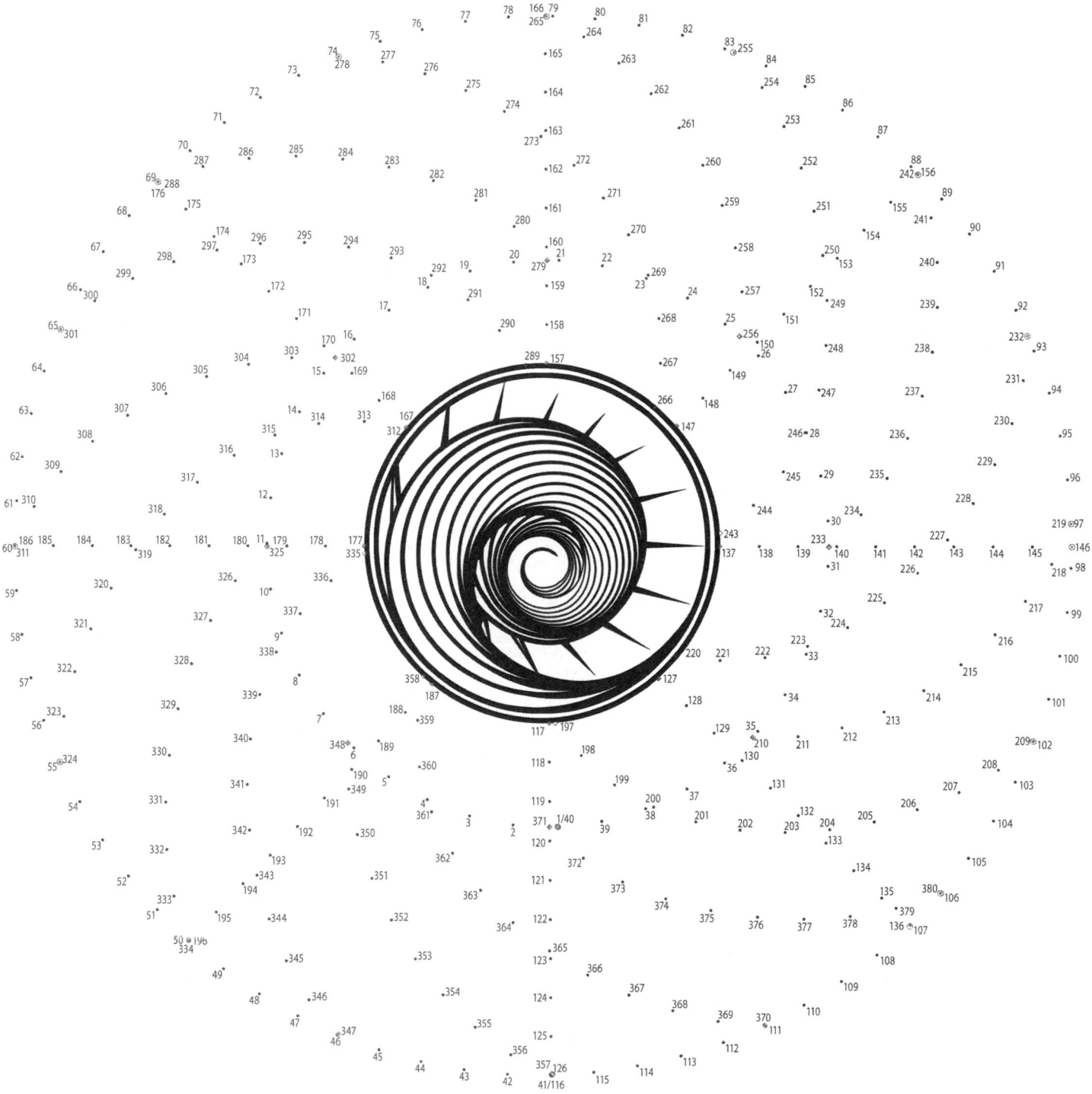

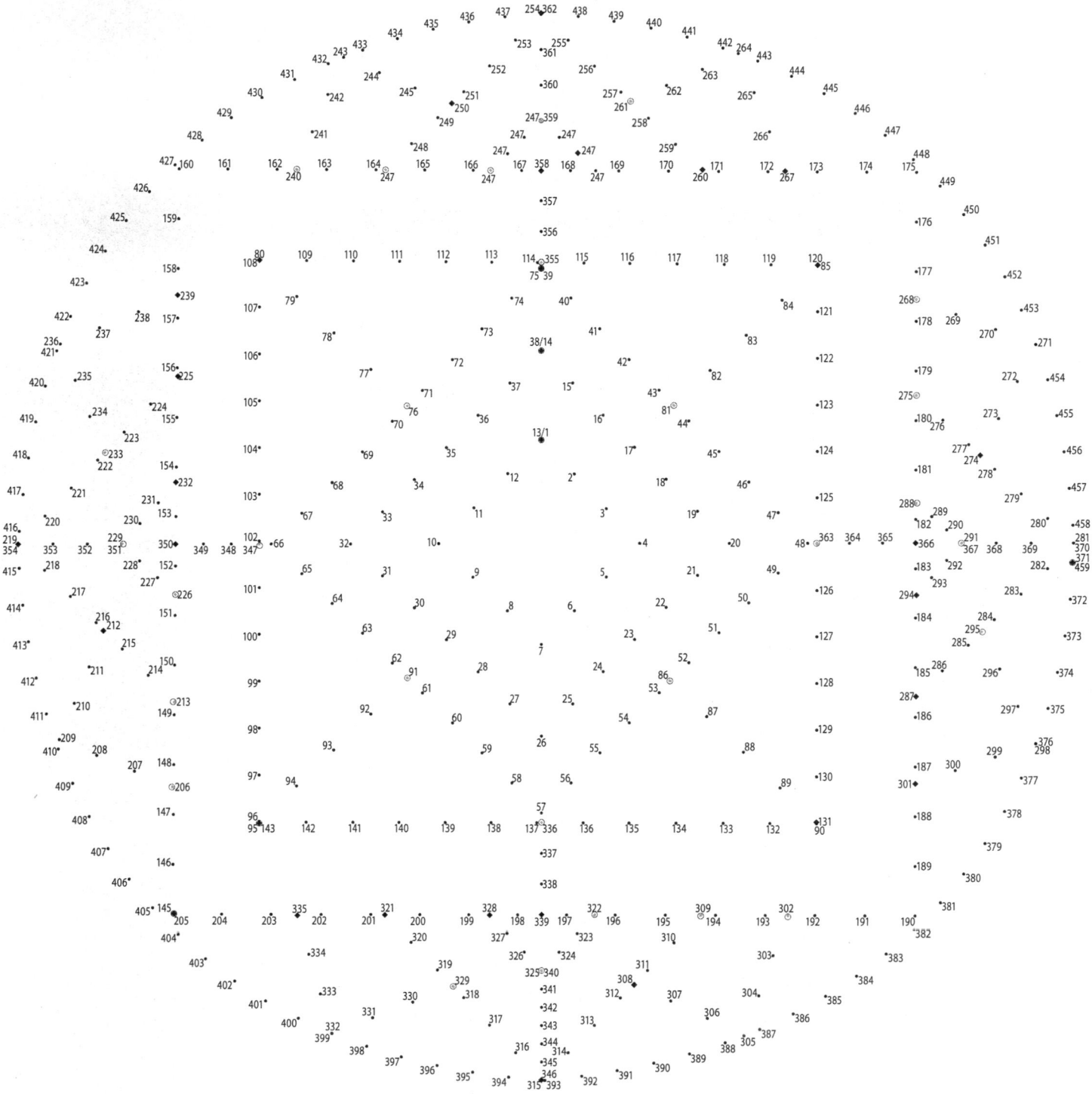

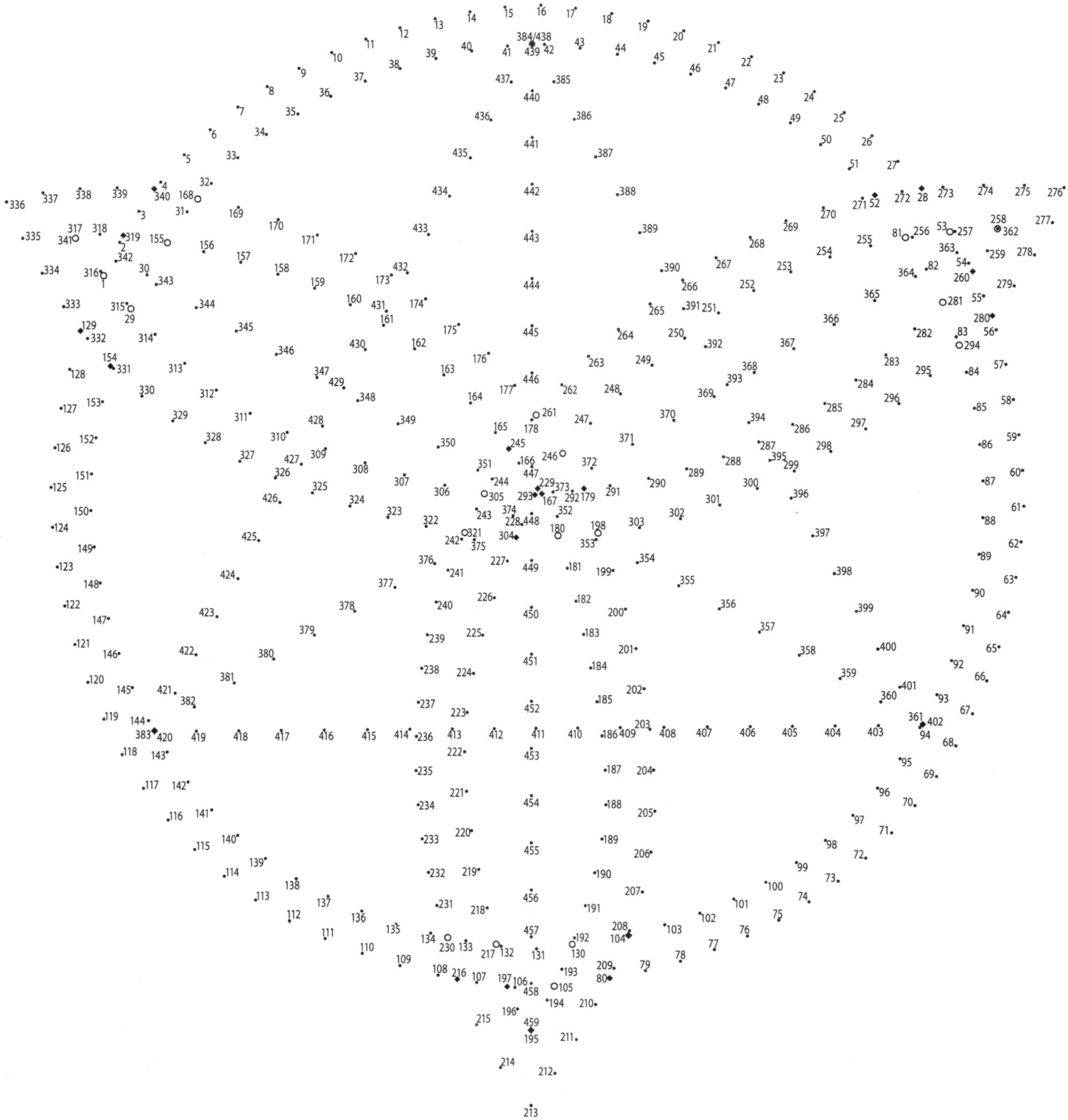

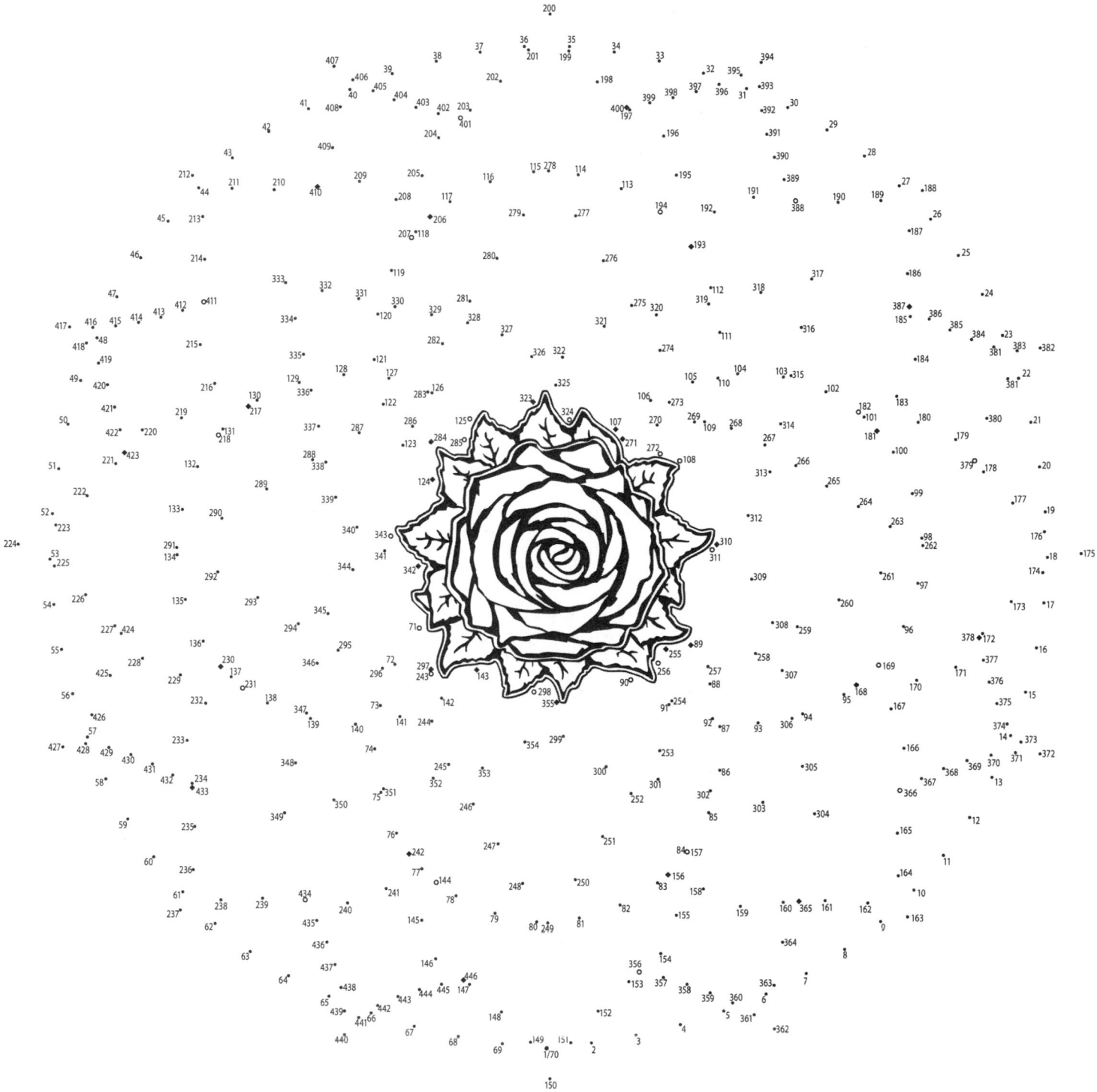

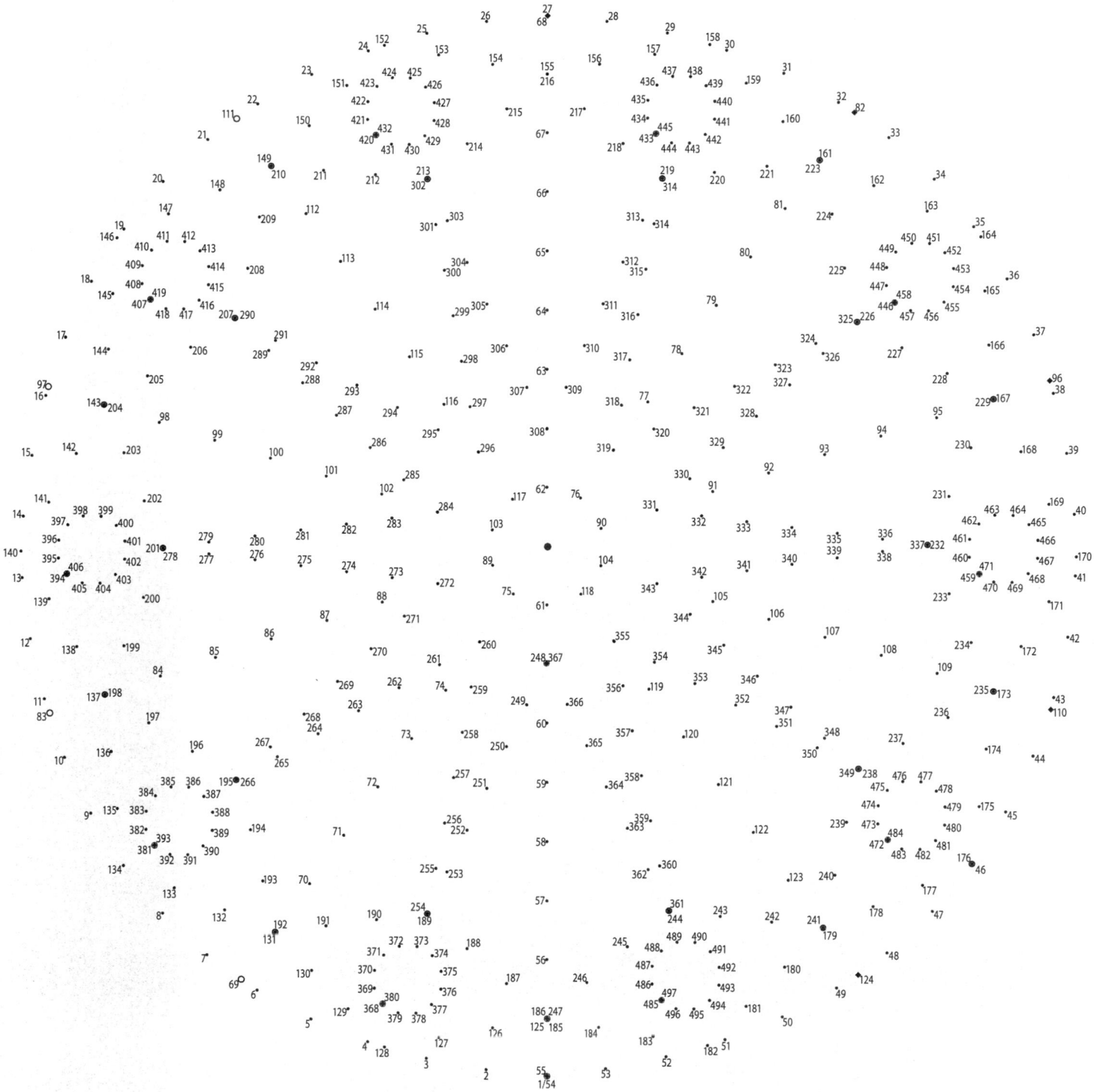

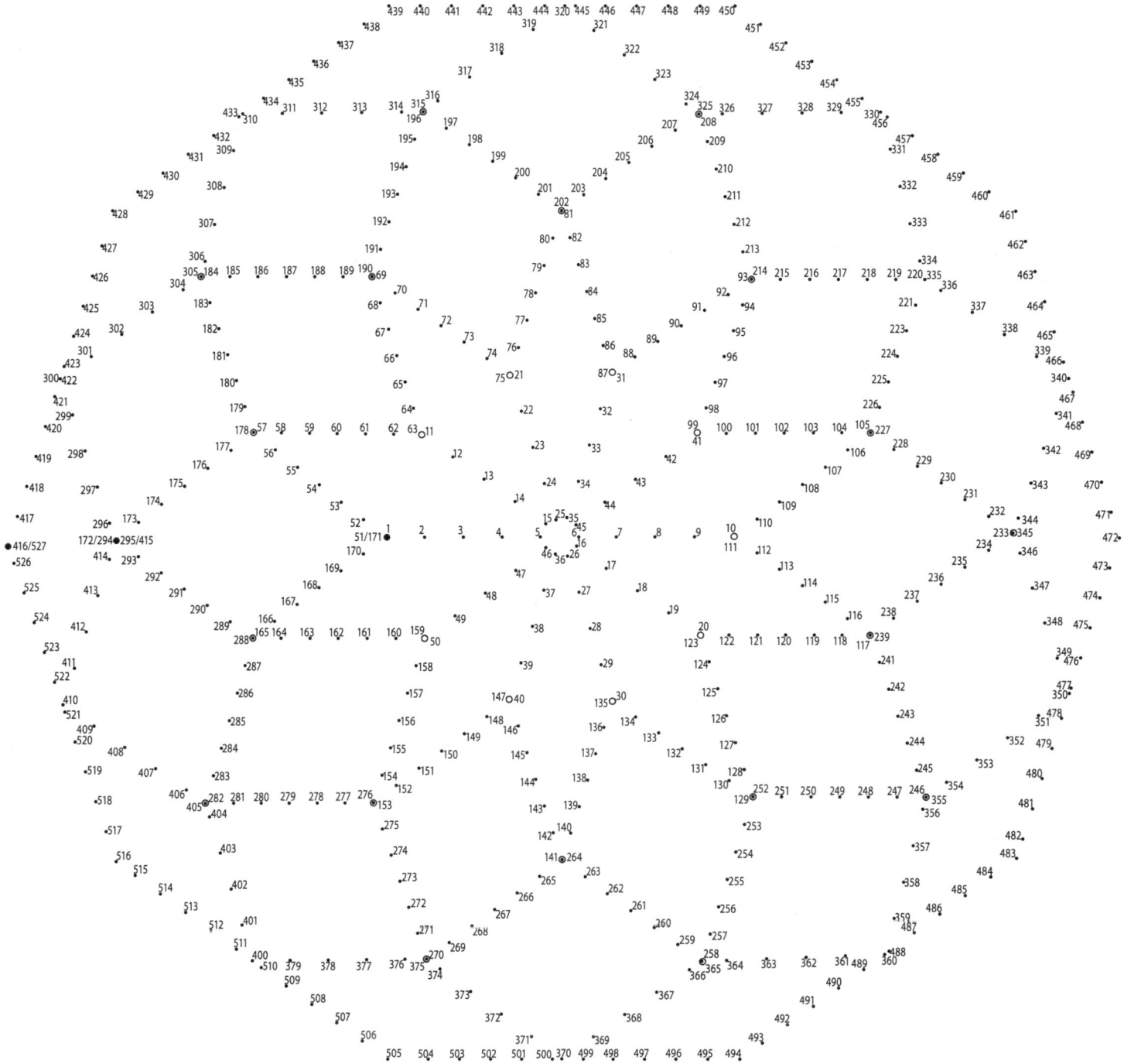

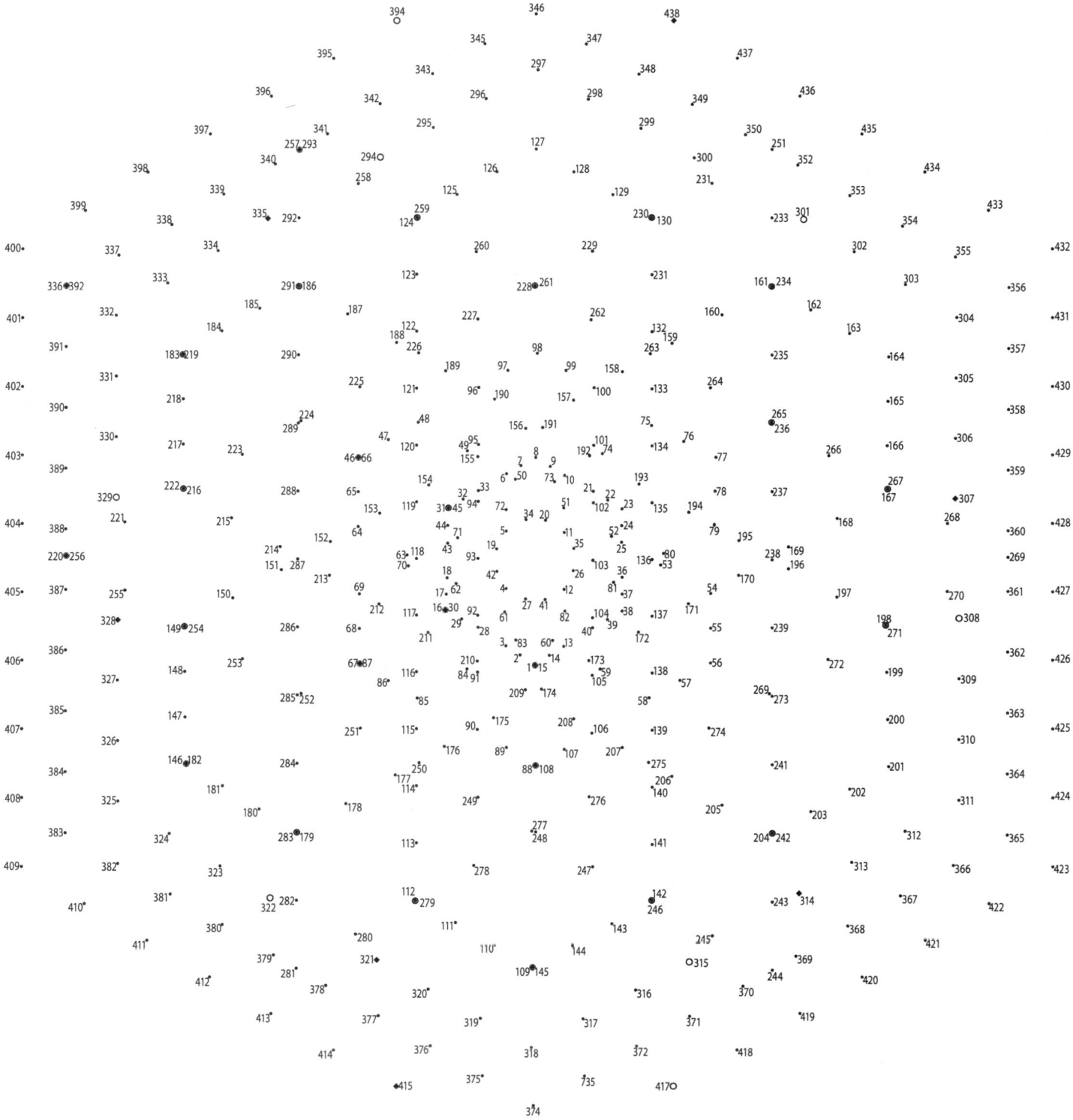

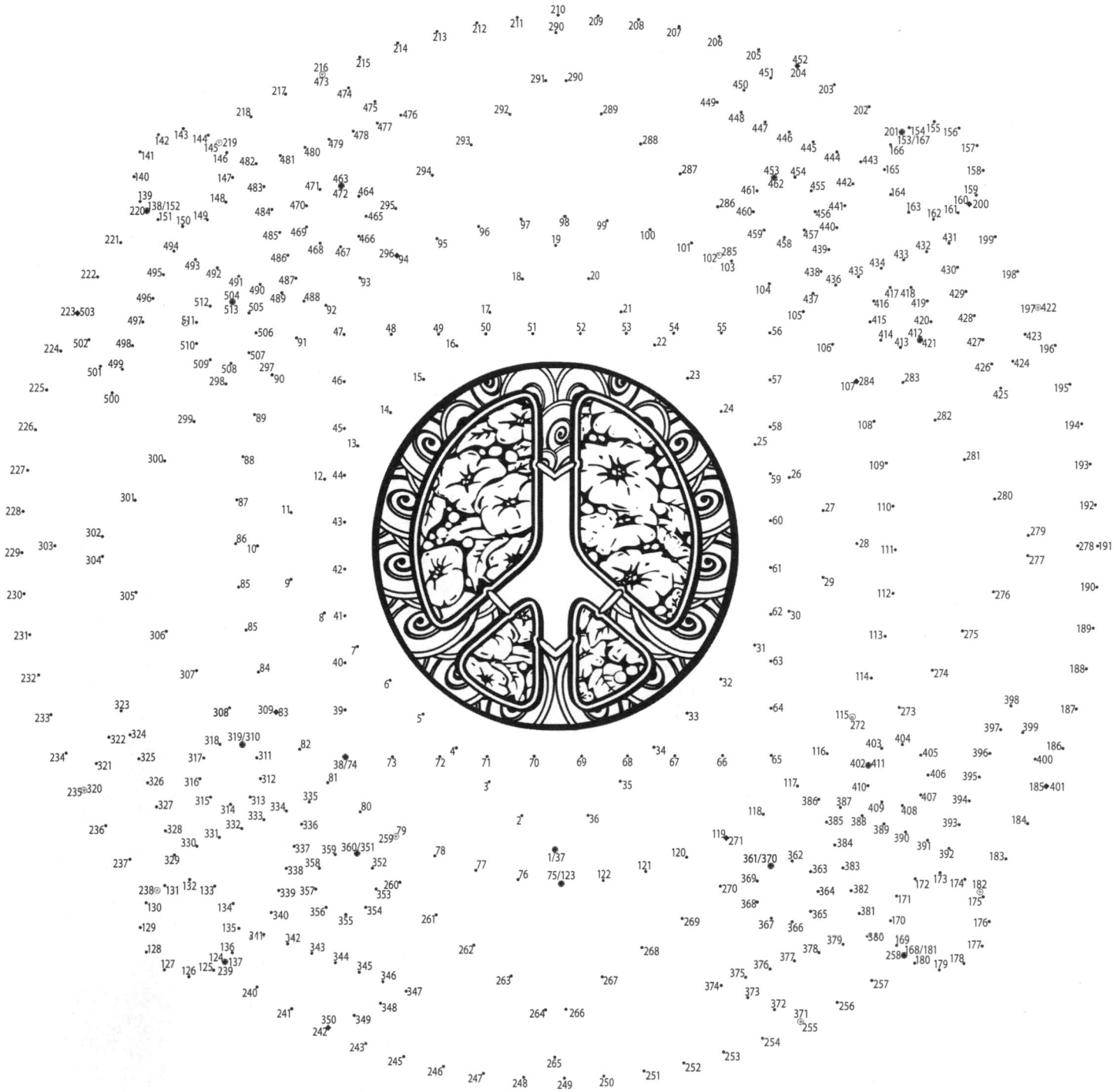

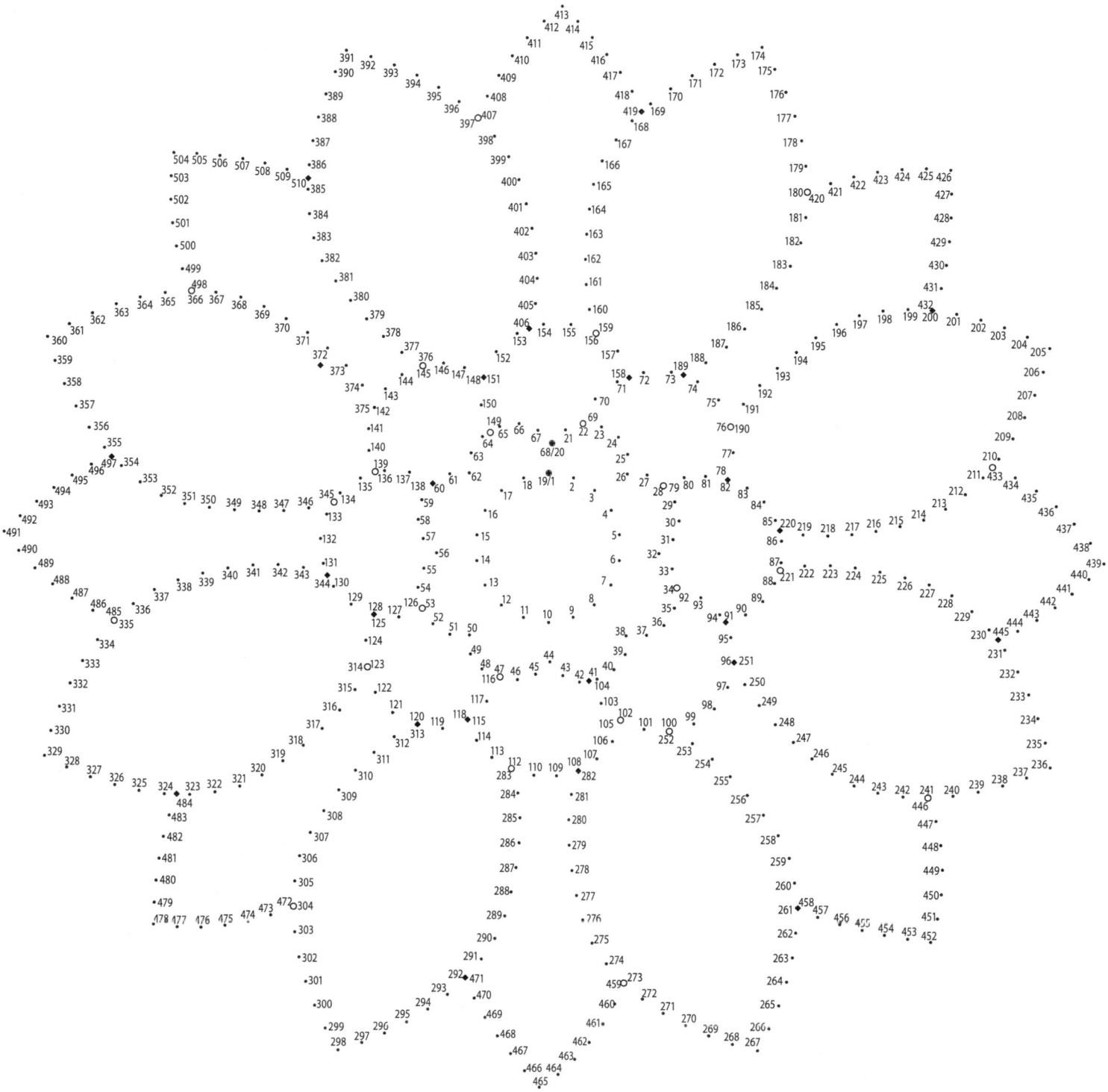

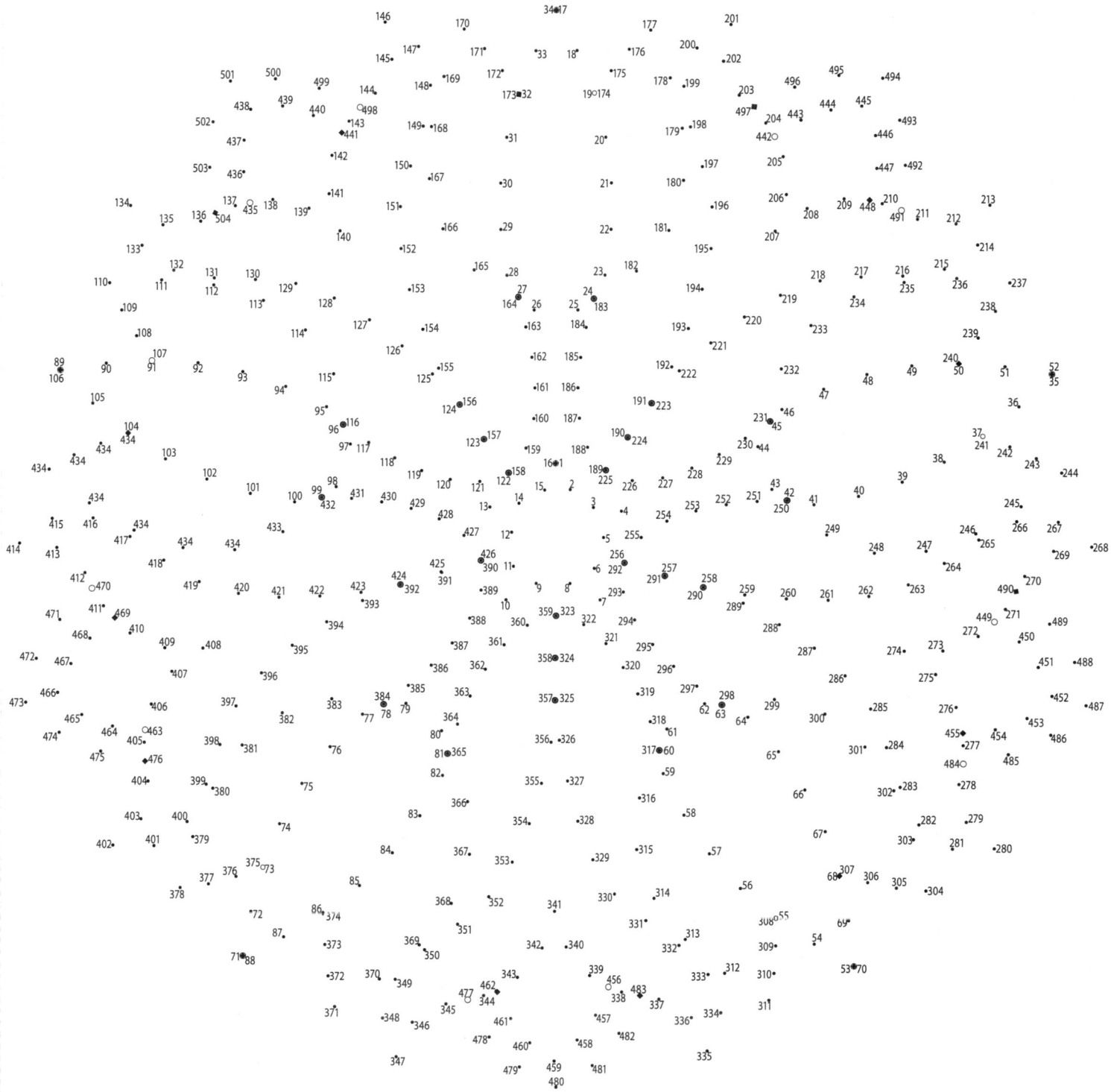

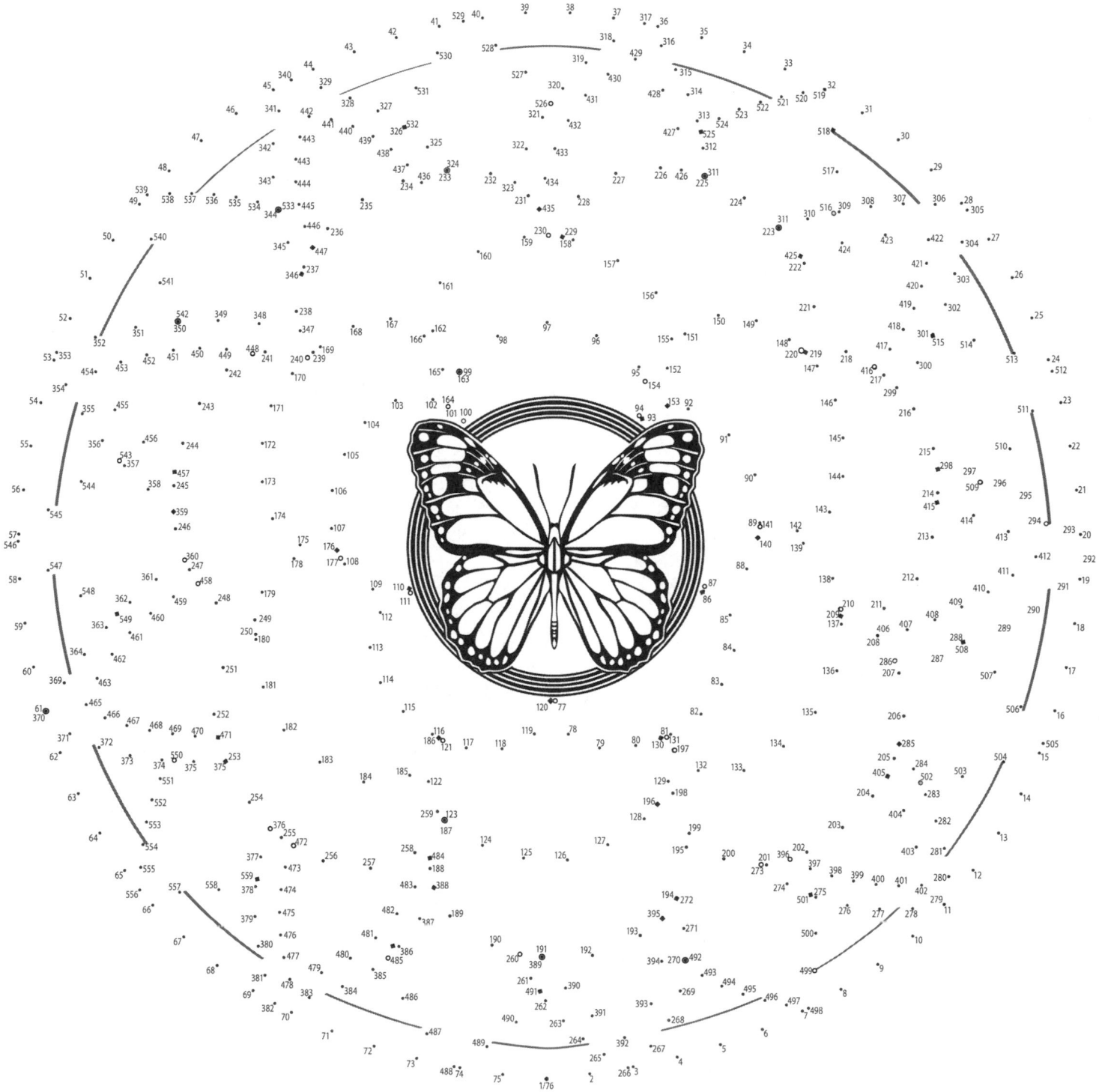

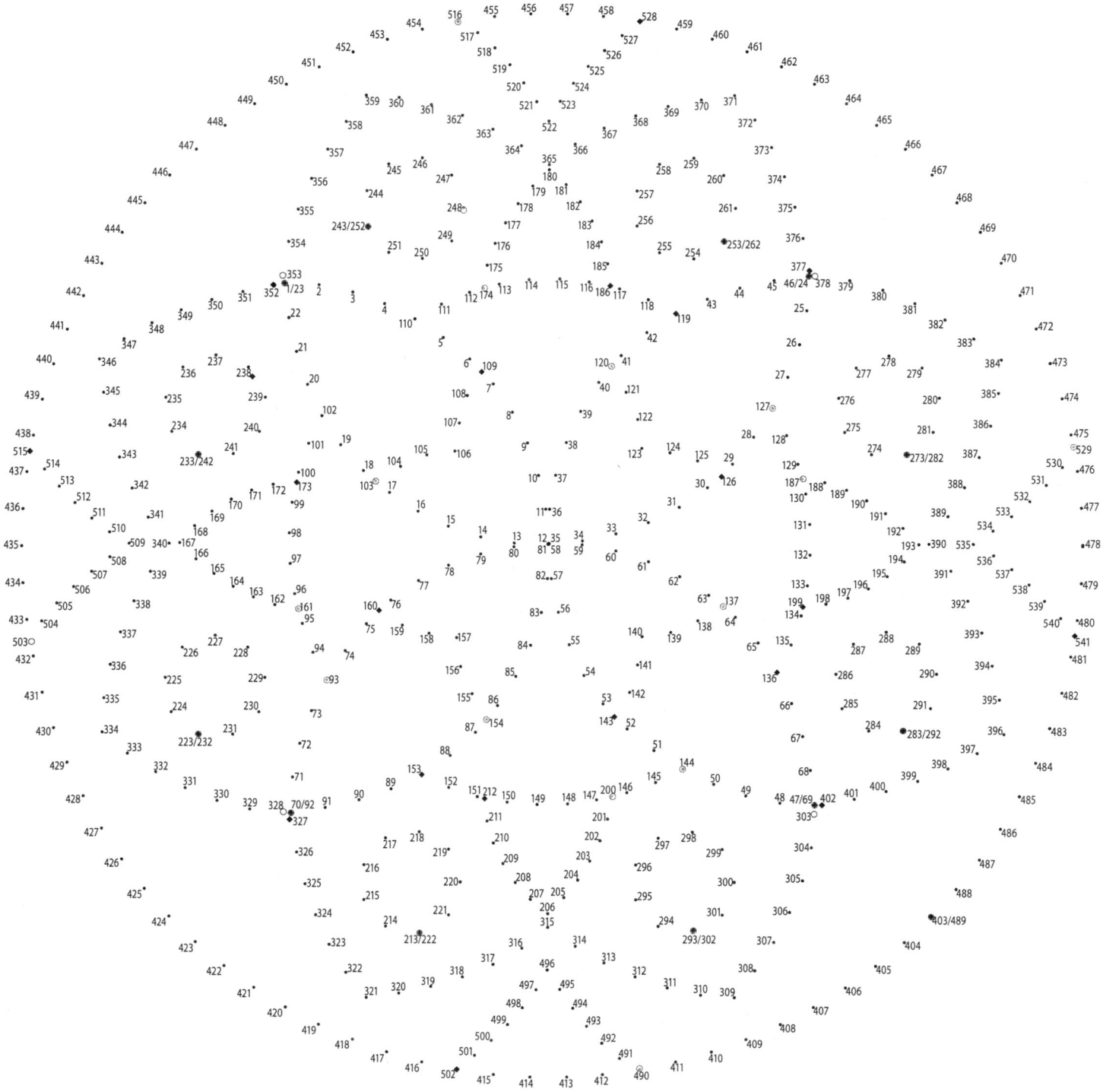

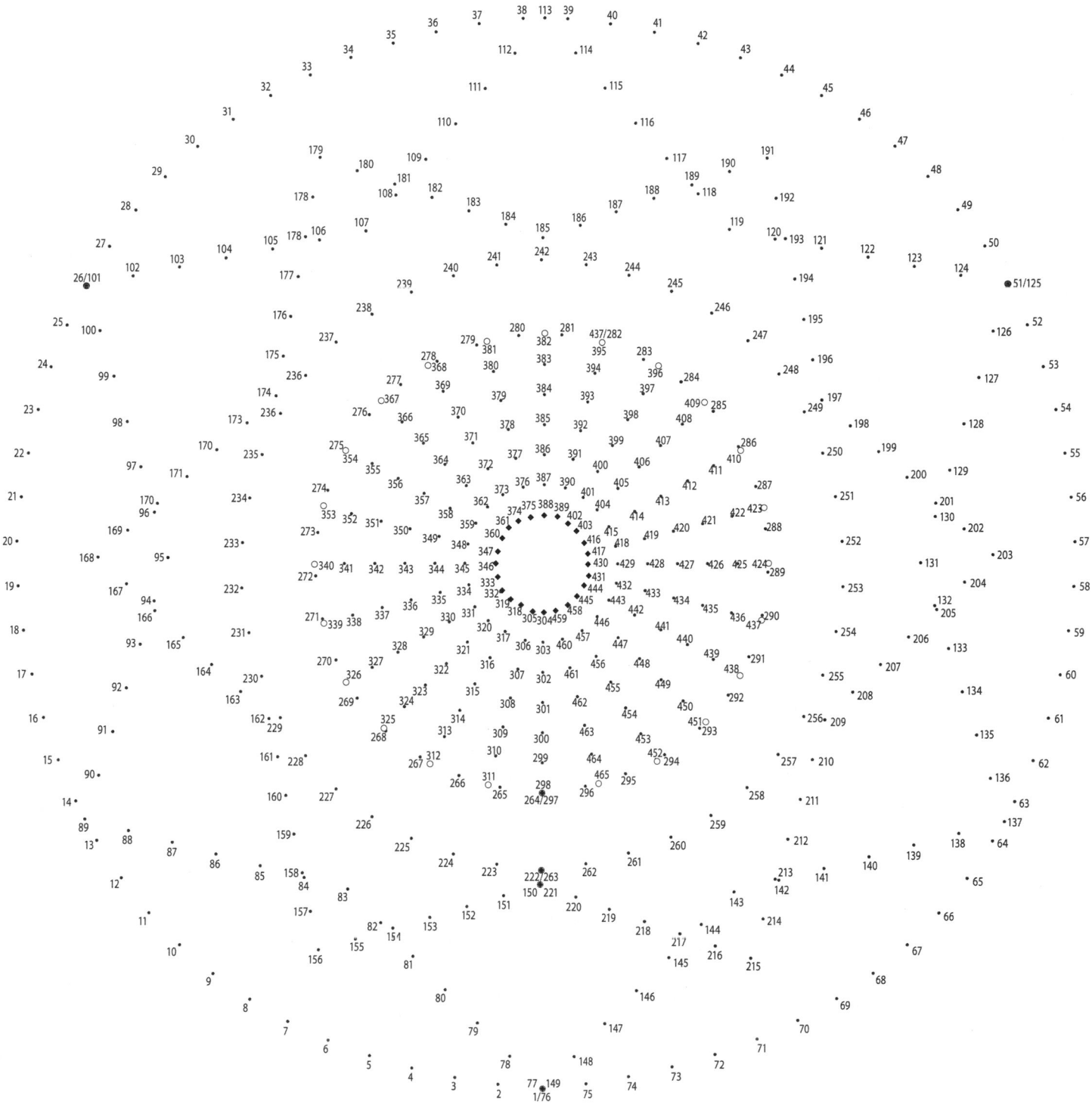

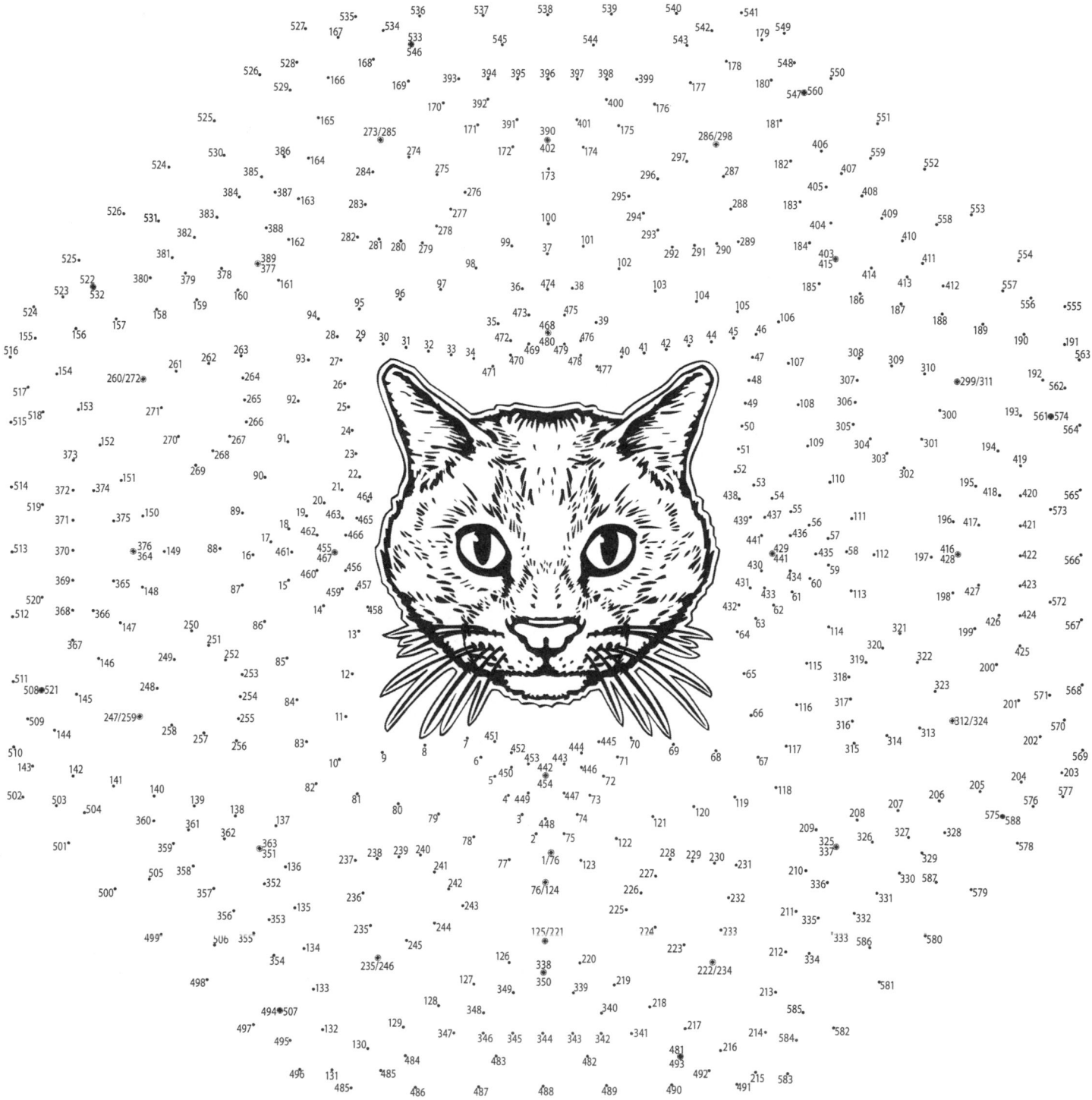

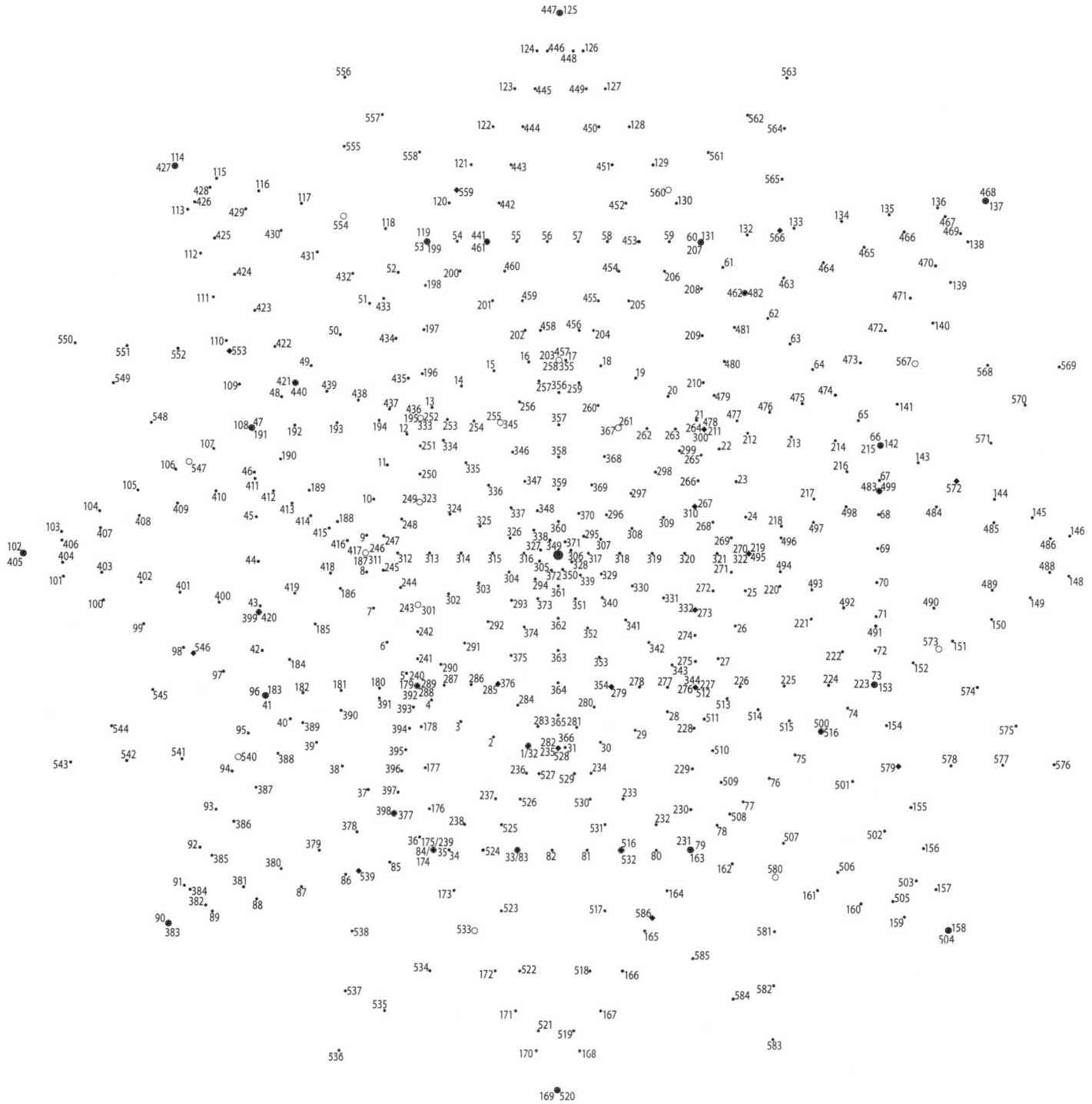

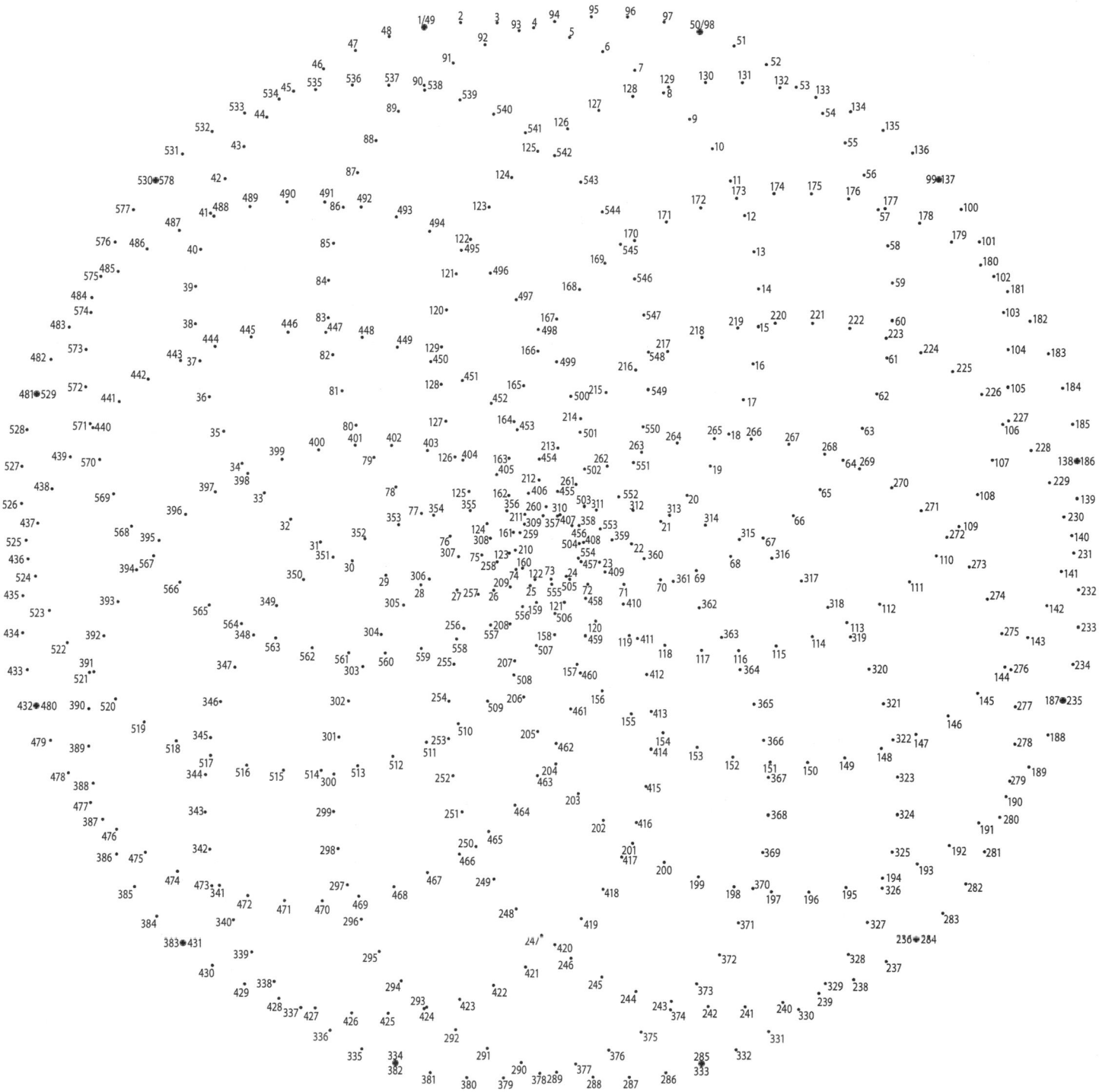

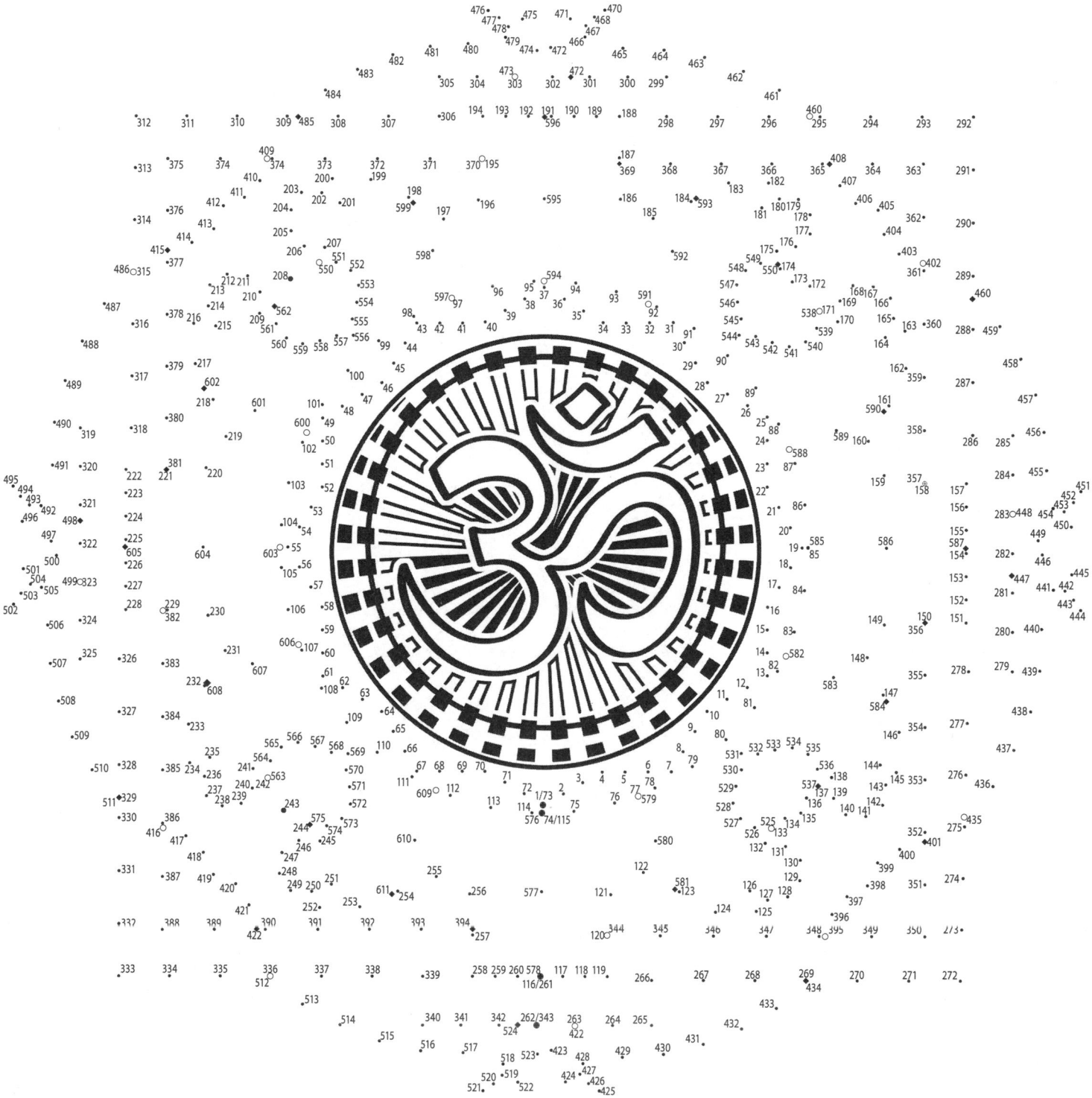

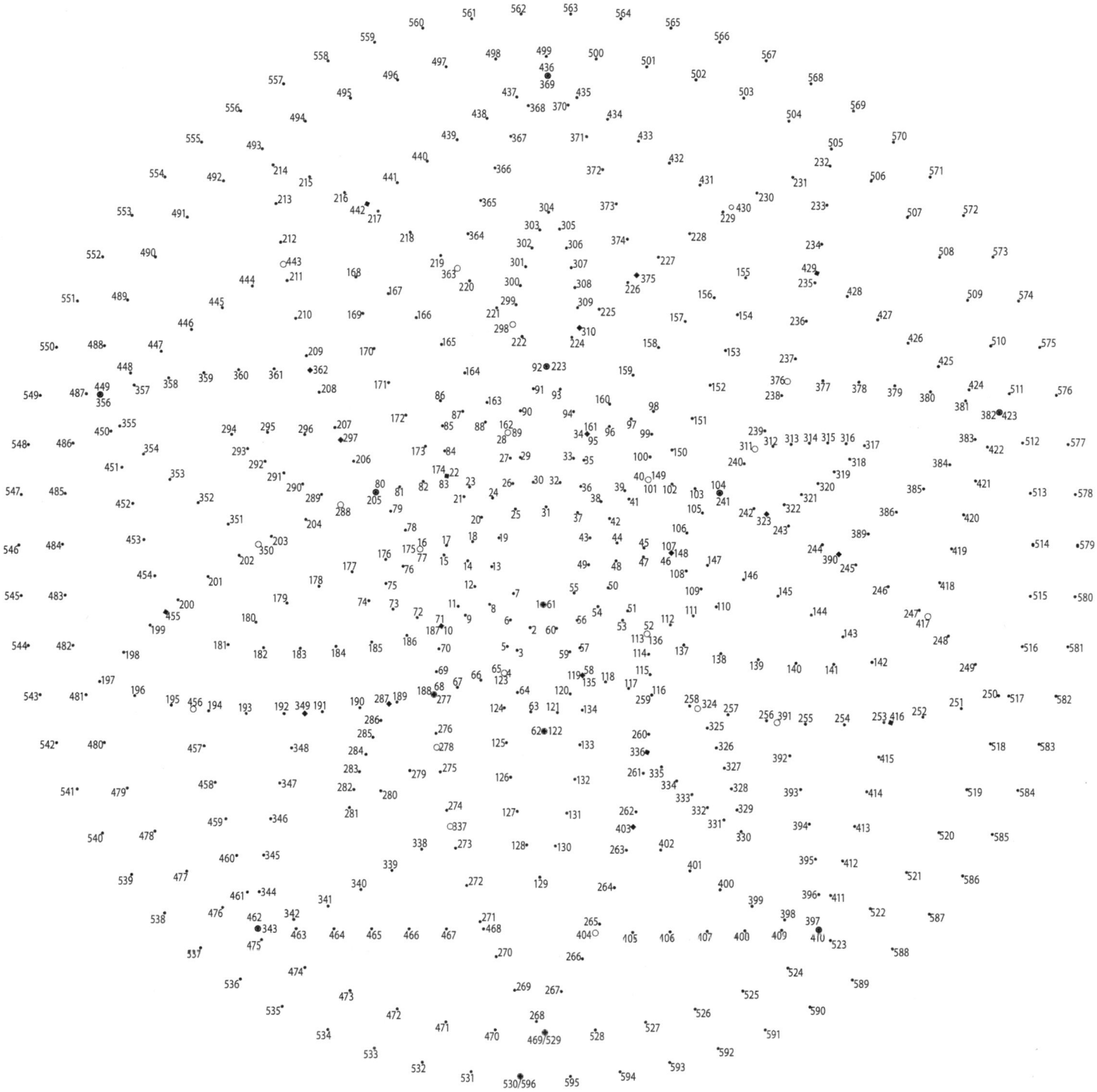

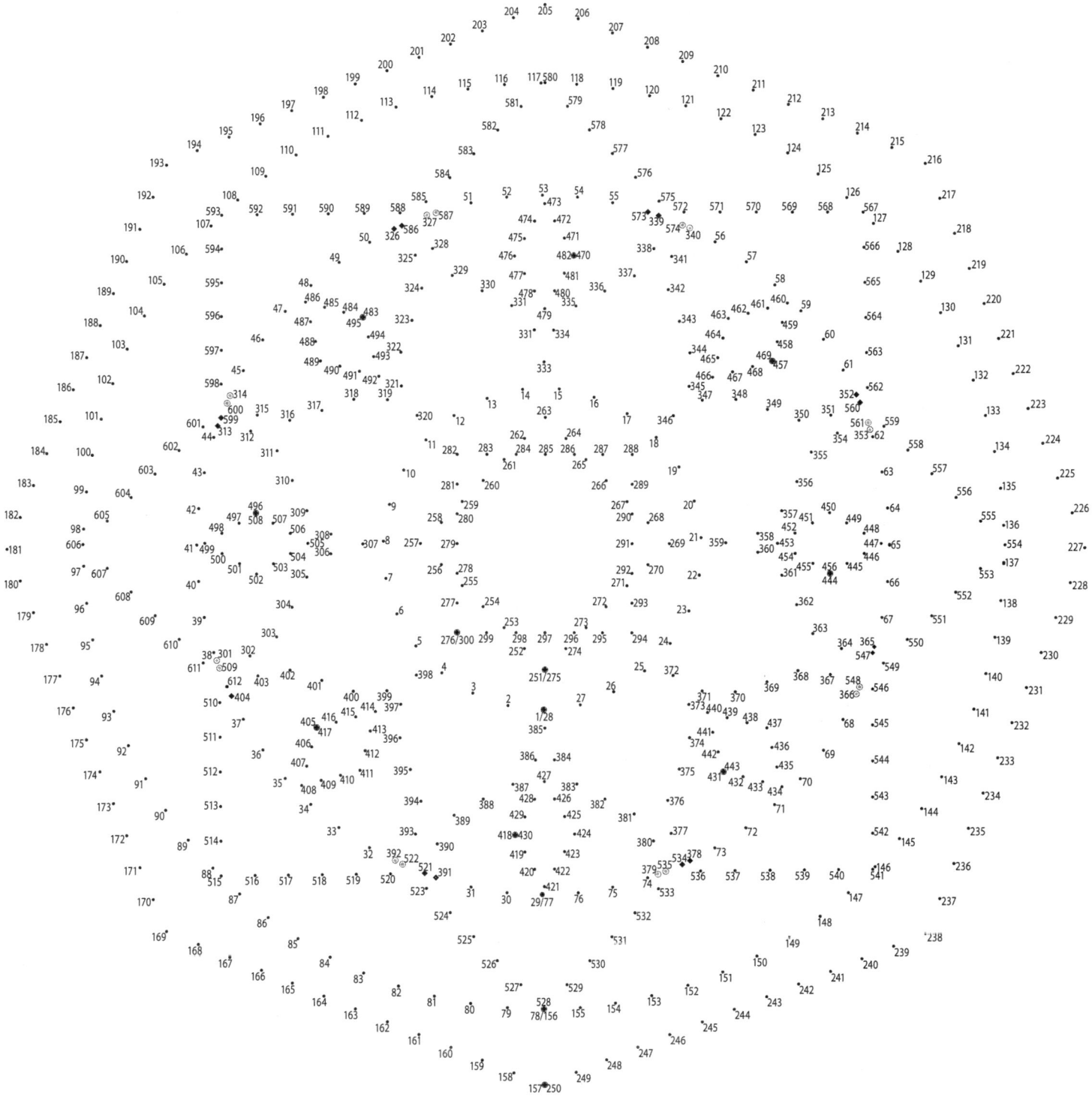

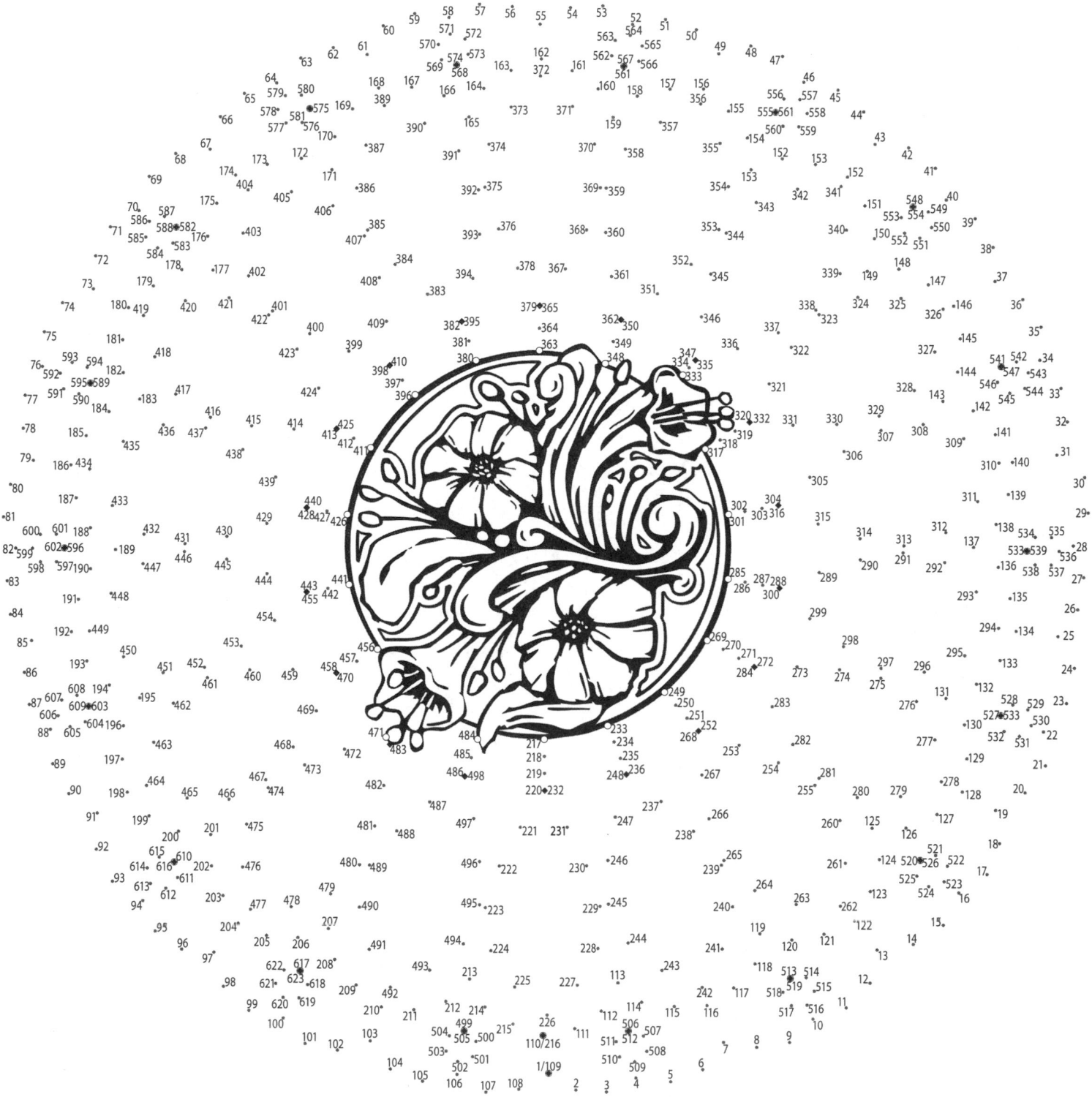

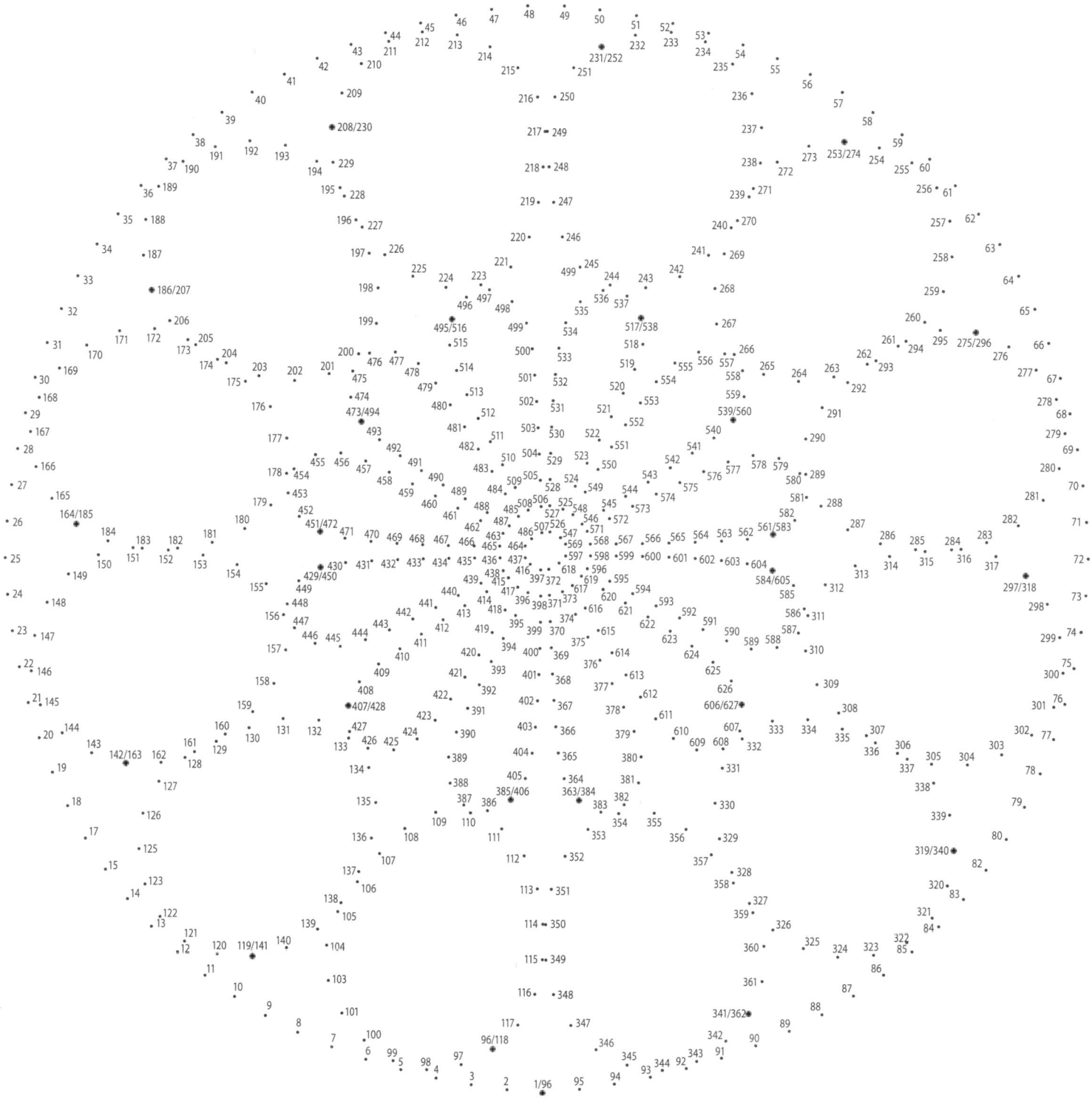
231/252
208/230
253/274
186/207
275/296
495/516
517/538
473/494
539/560
164/185
451/472
561/583
429/450
584/605
297/318
407/428
606/627
142/163
385/406
363/384
319/340
119/141
341/362
96/118
1/96

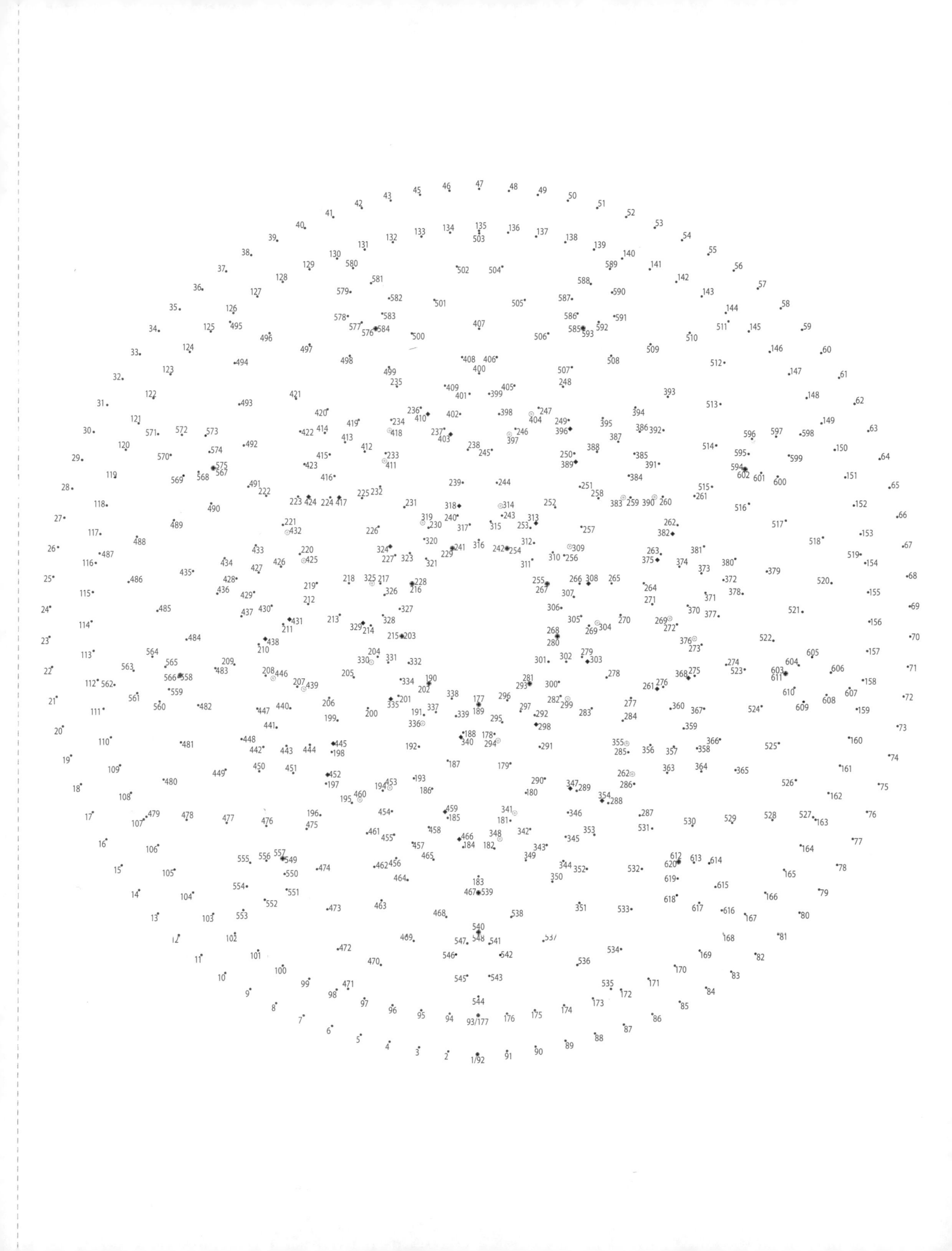

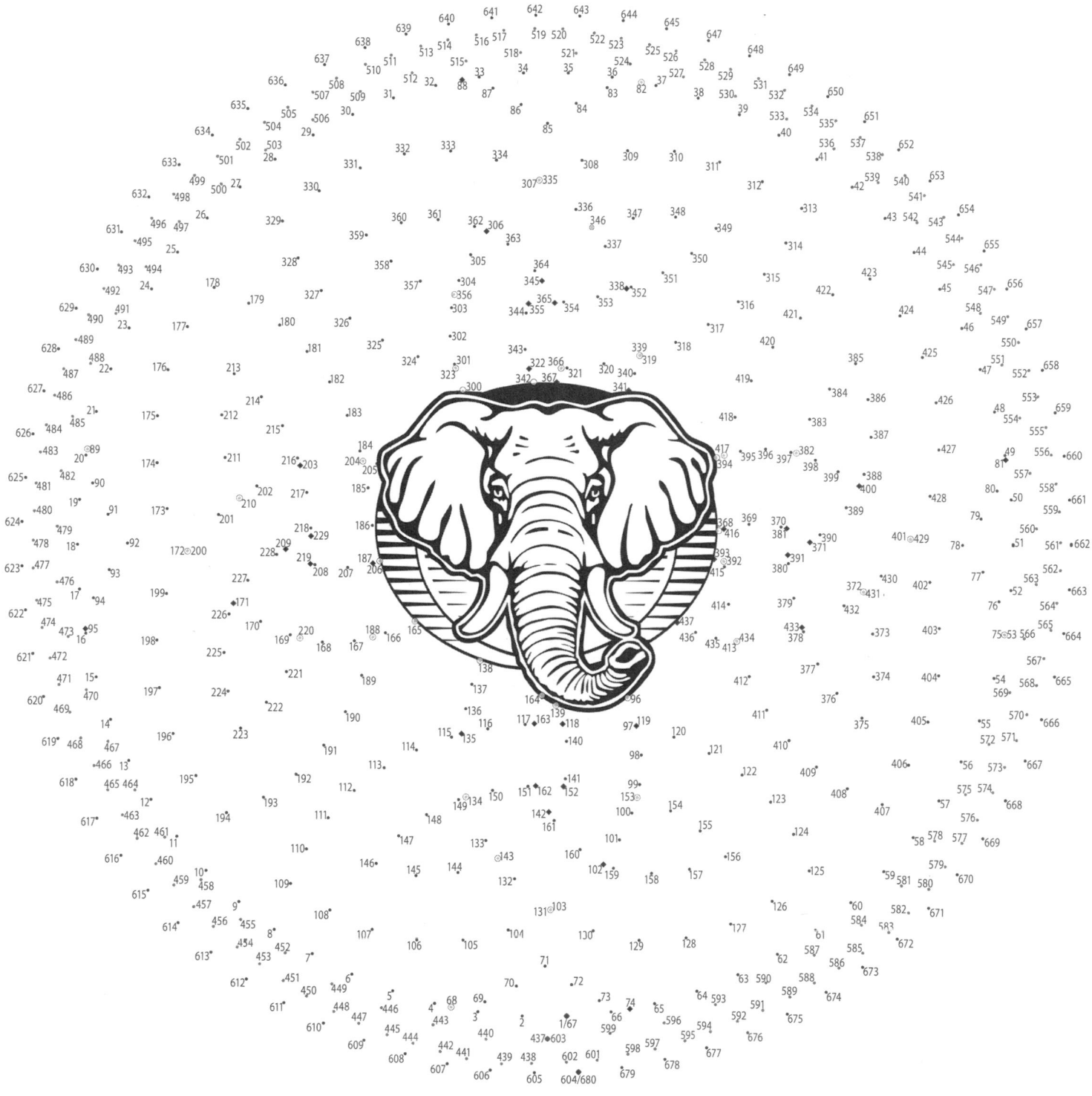

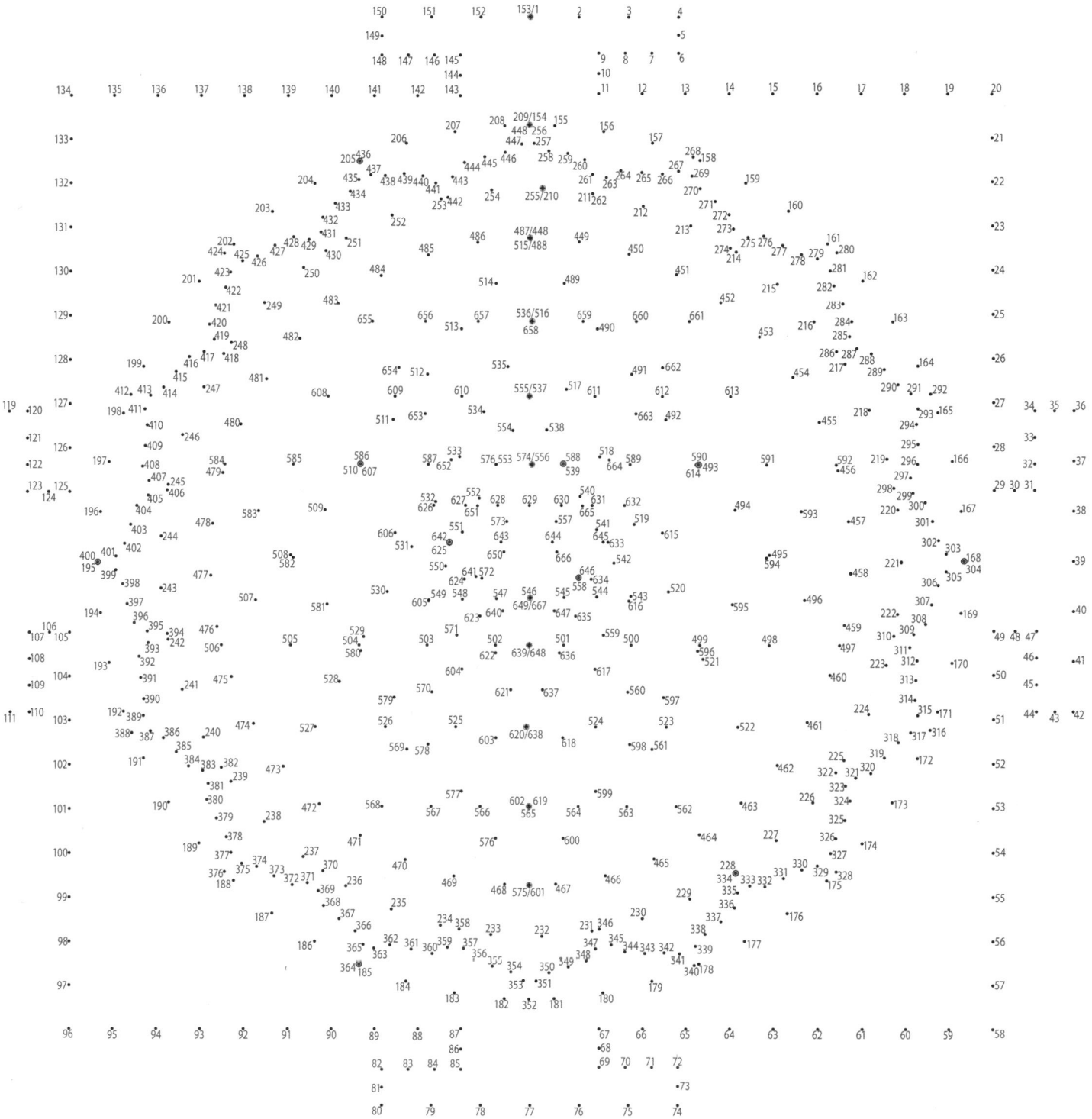

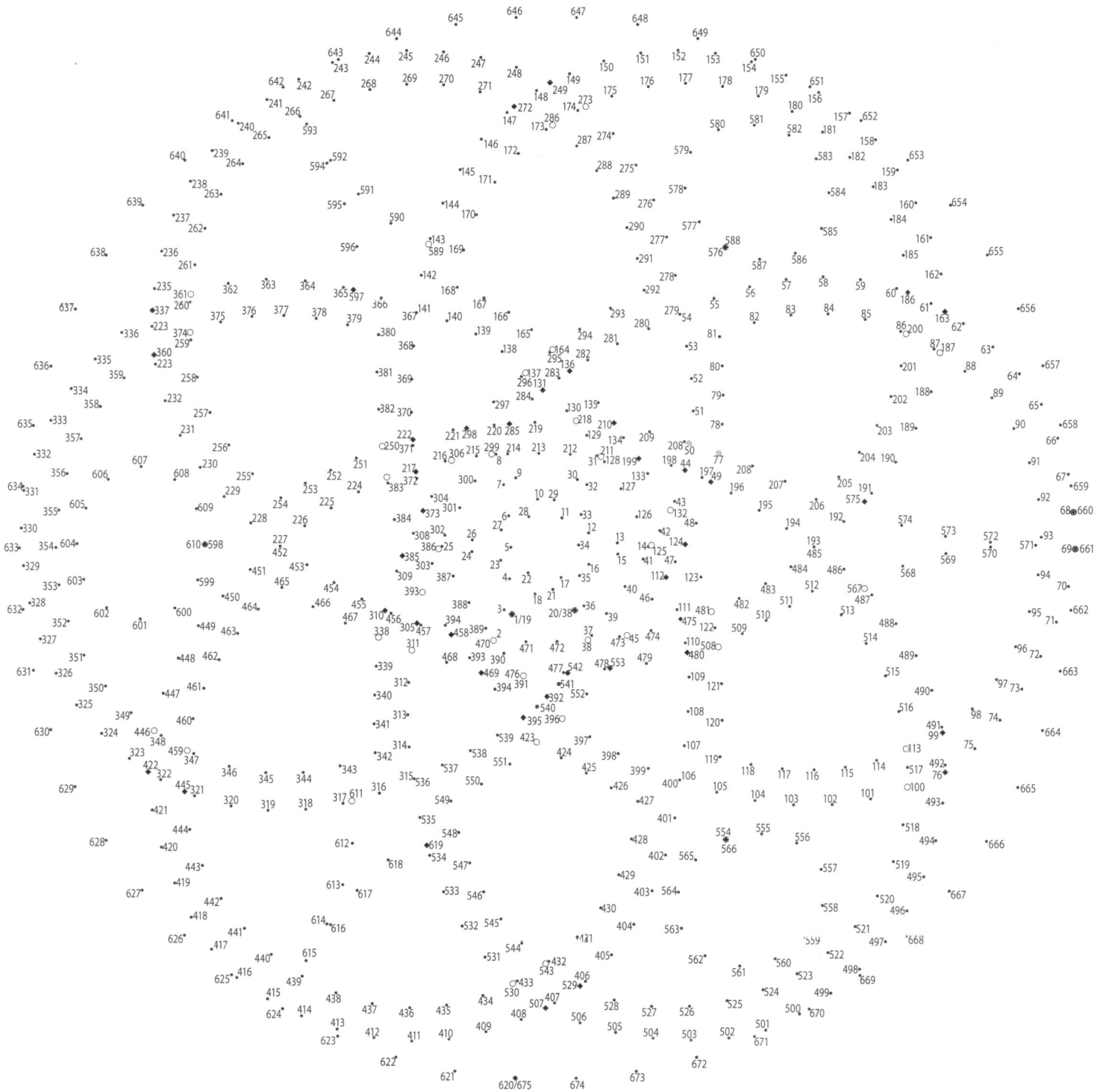

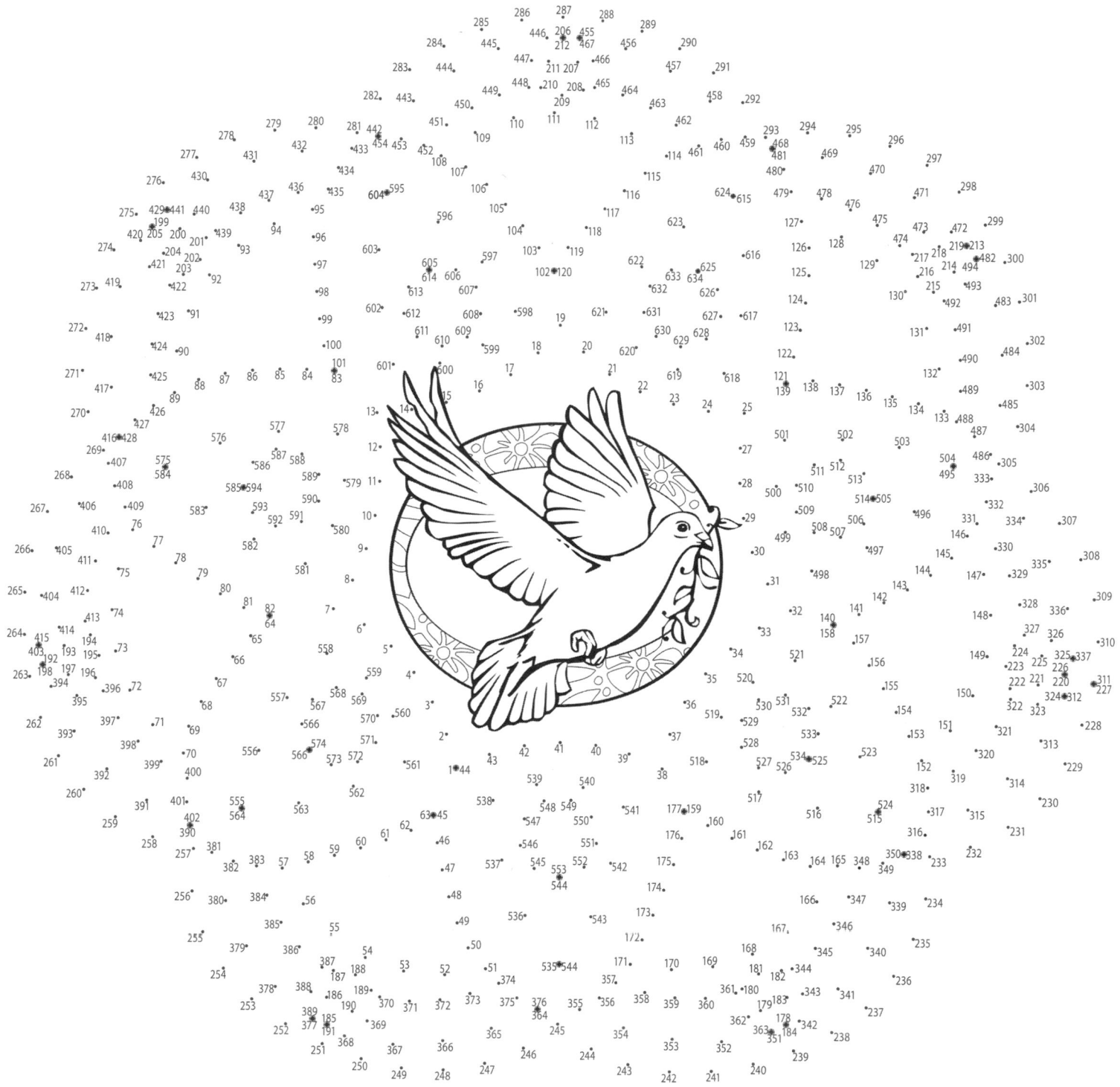

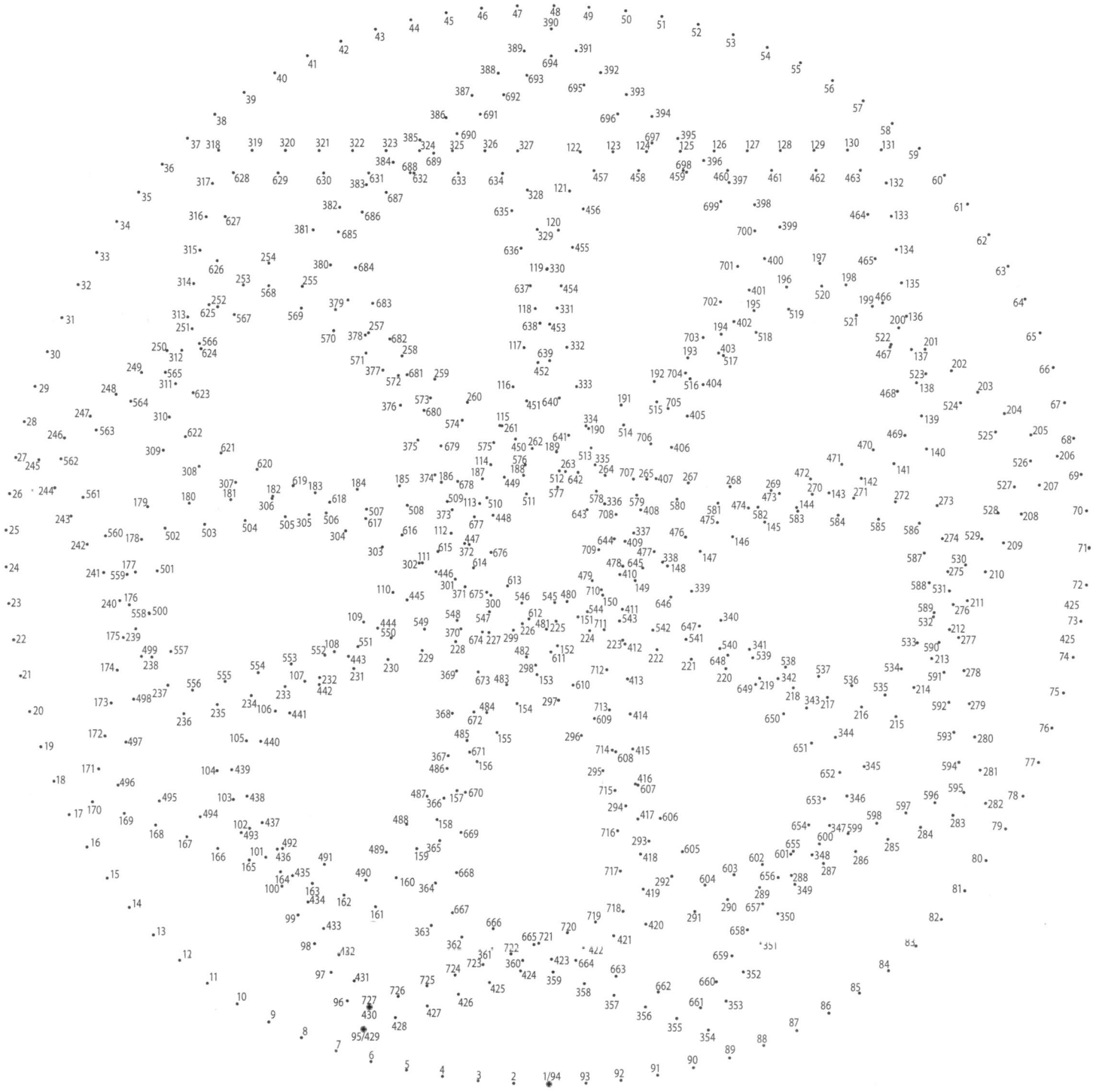

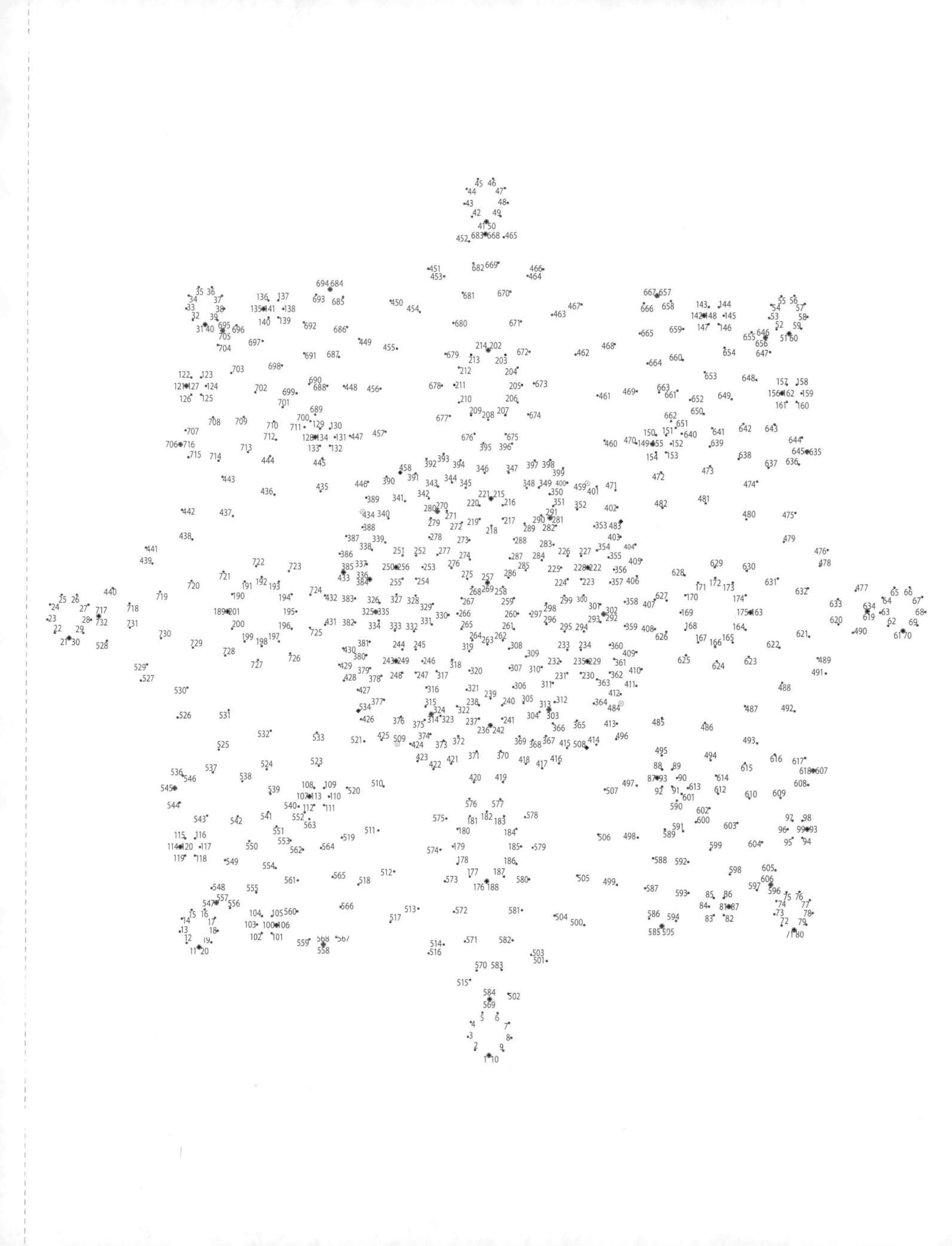

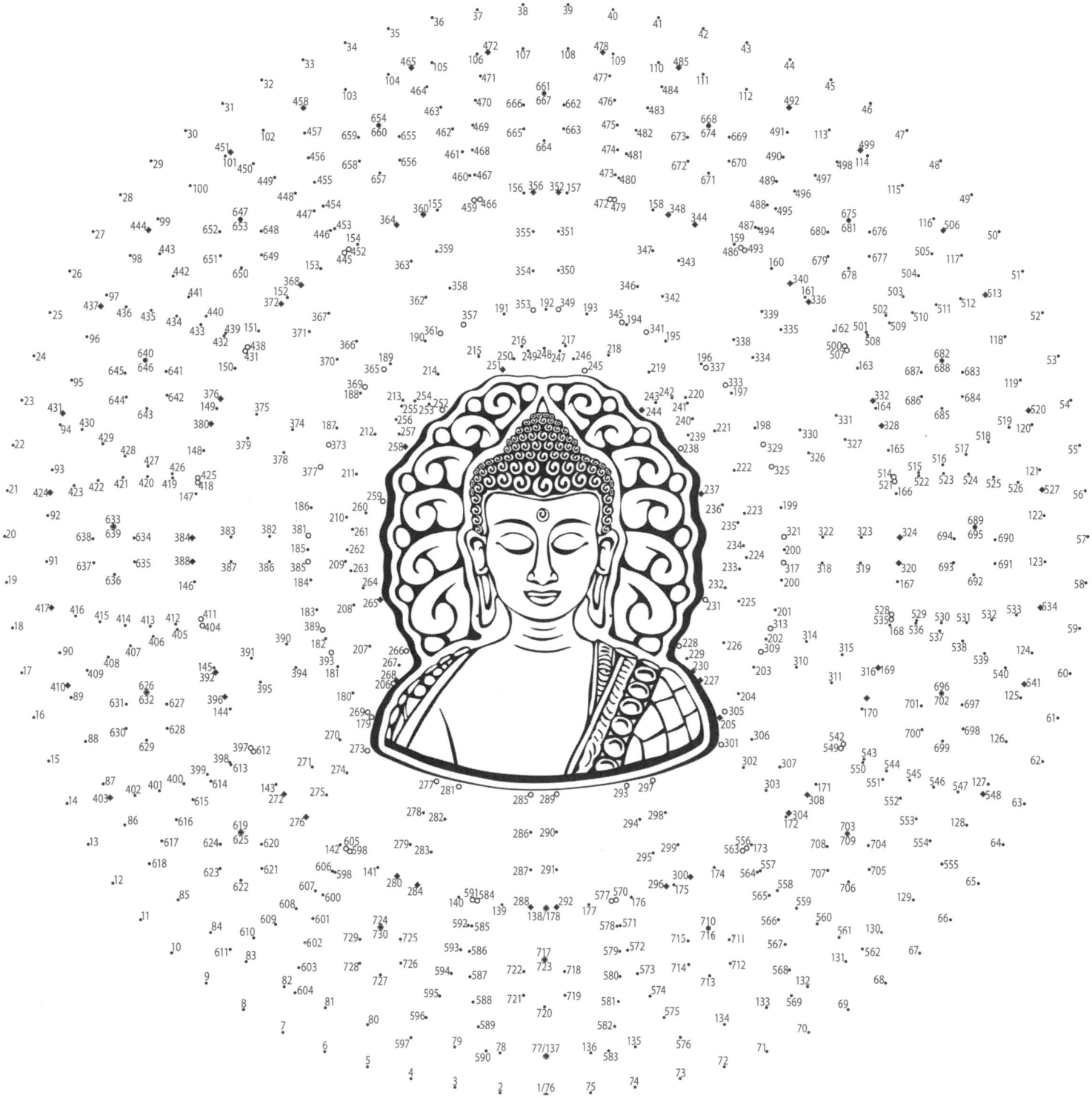

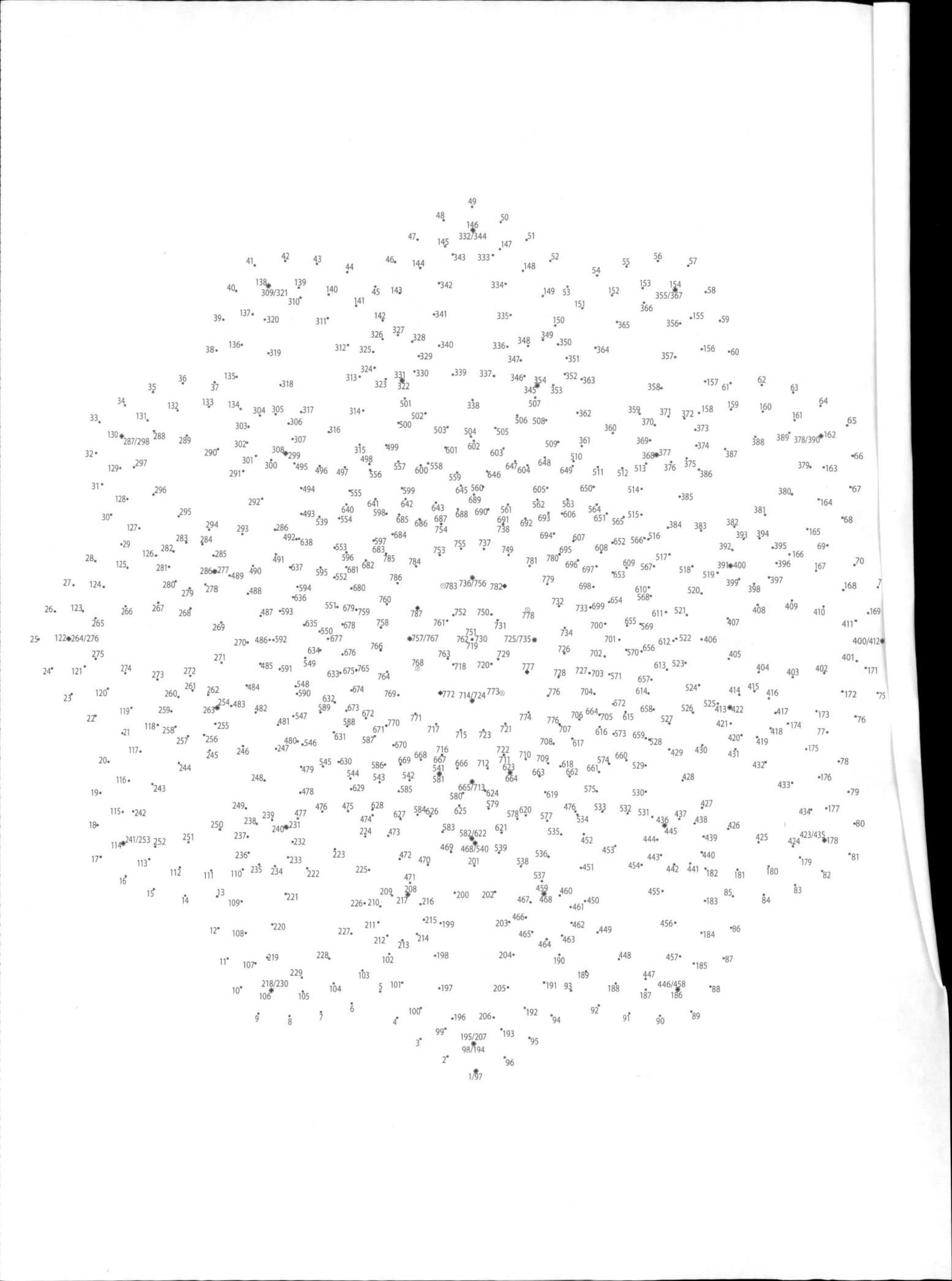

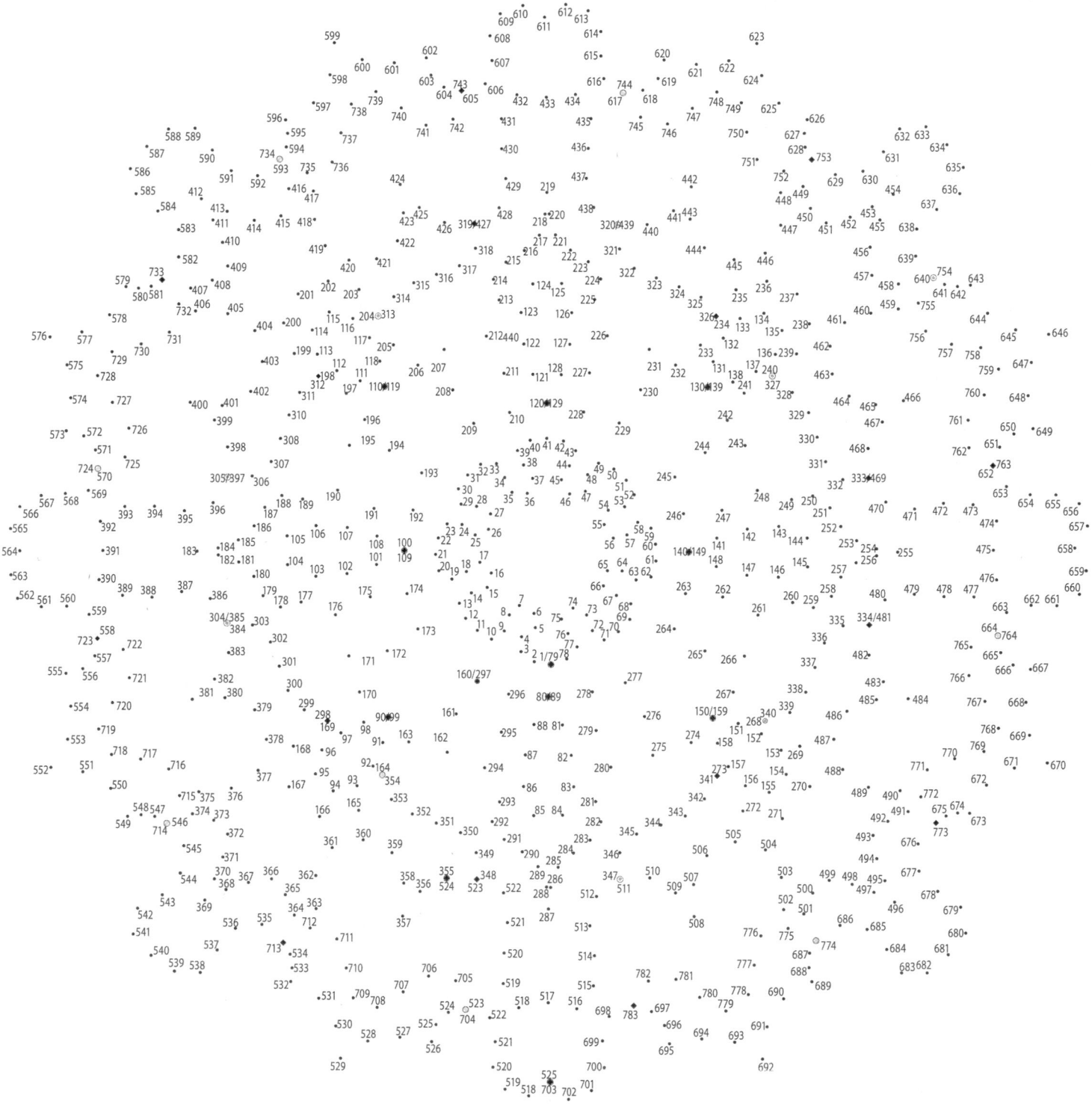

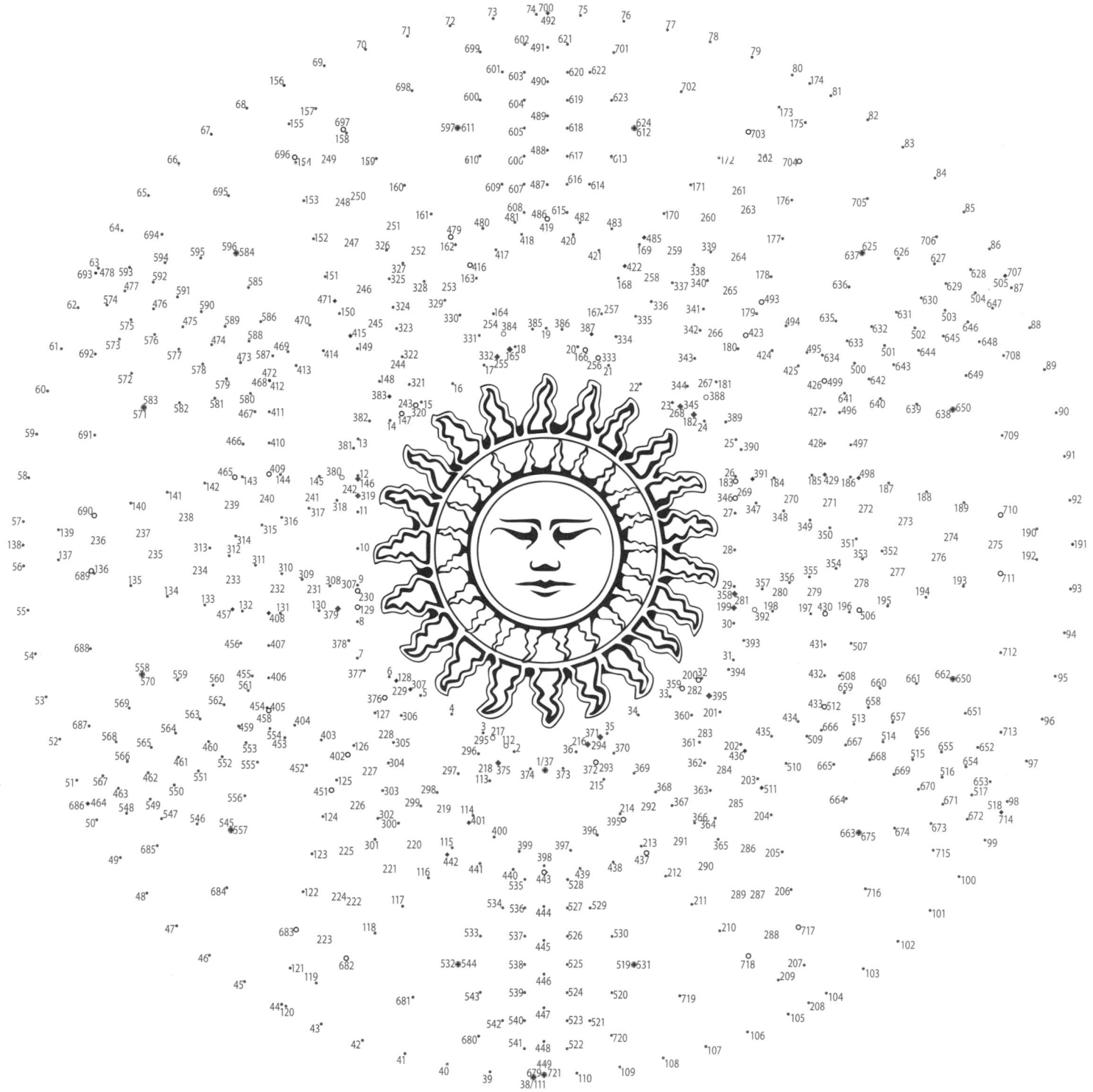

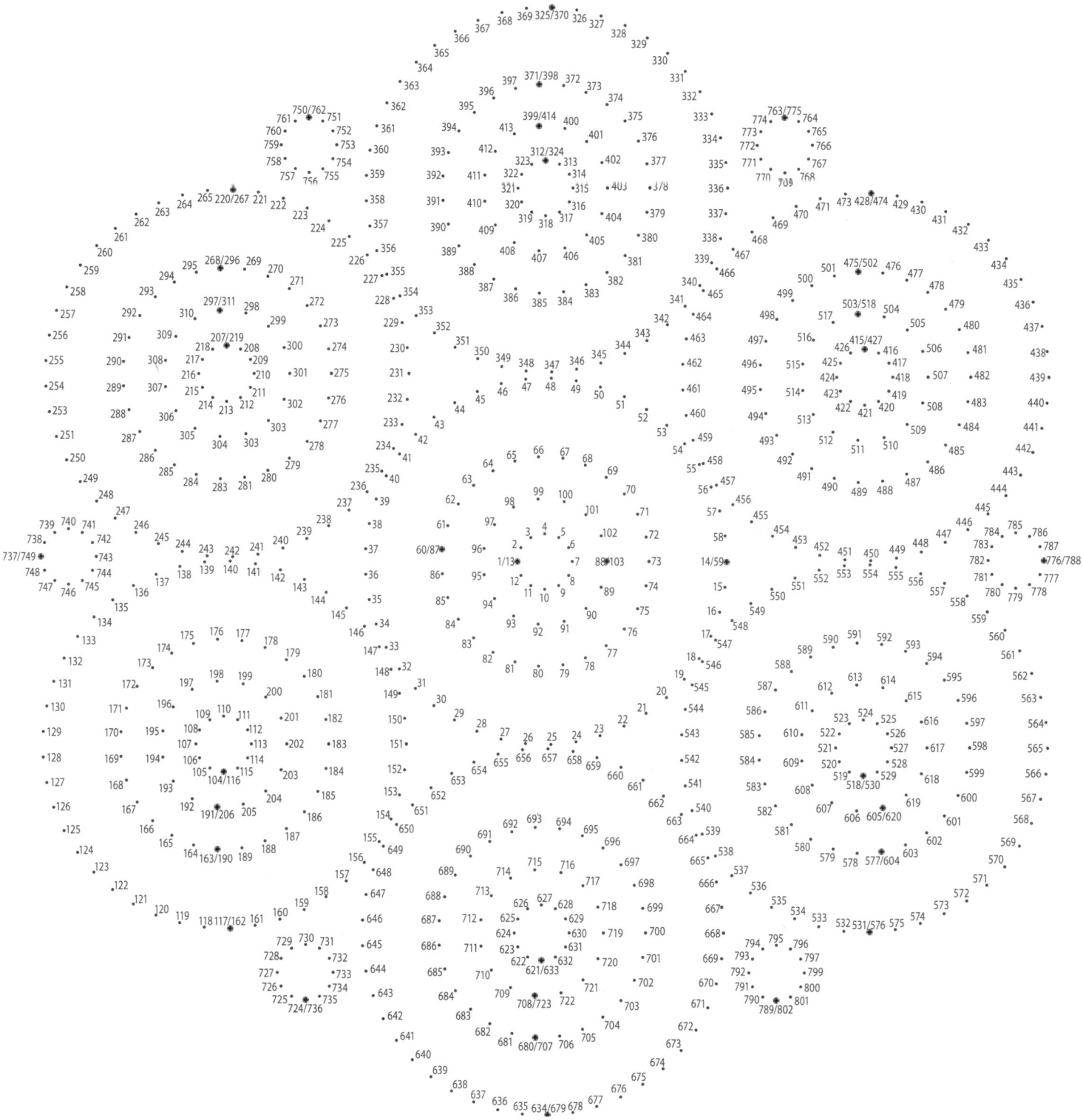

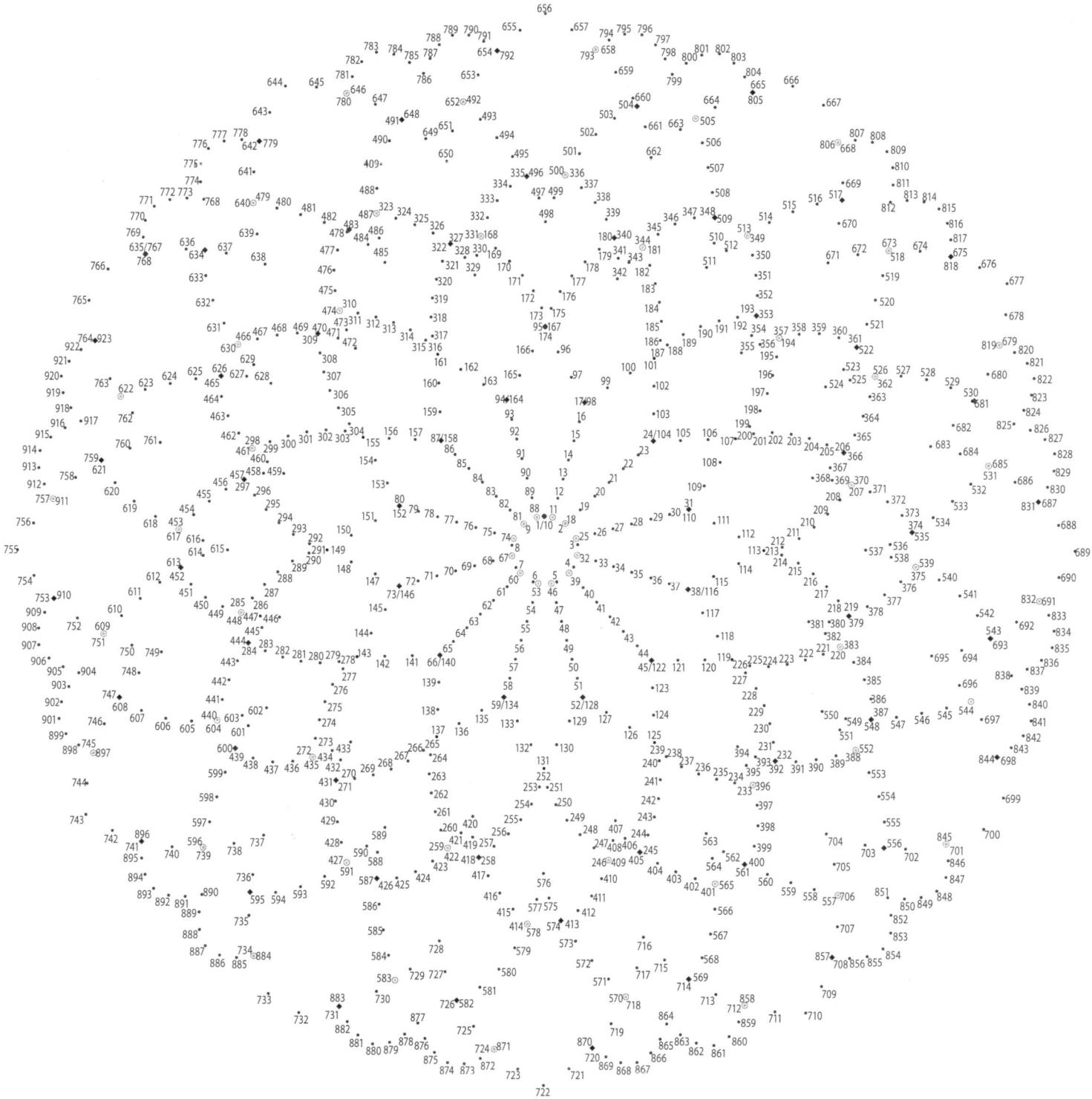

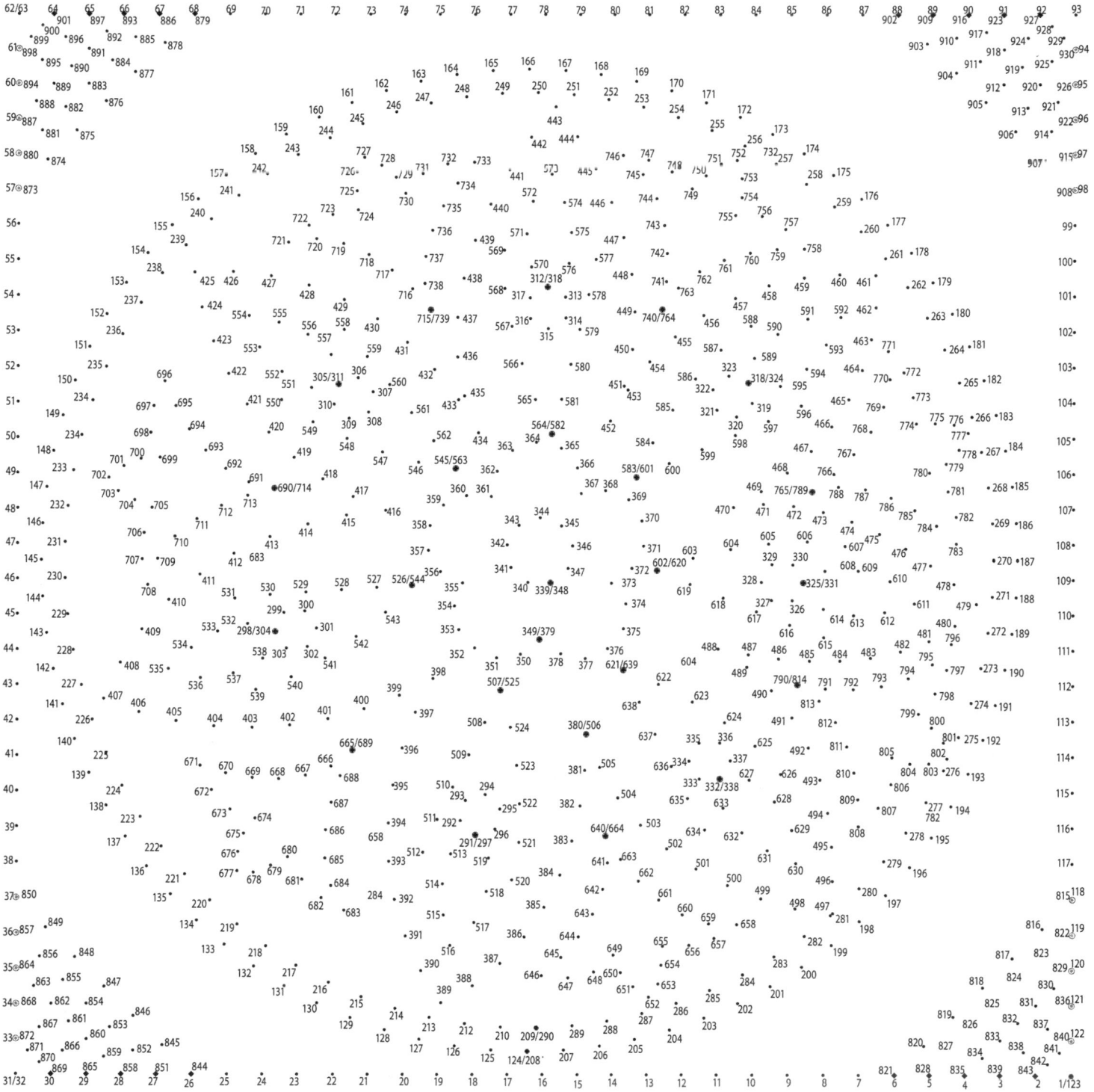

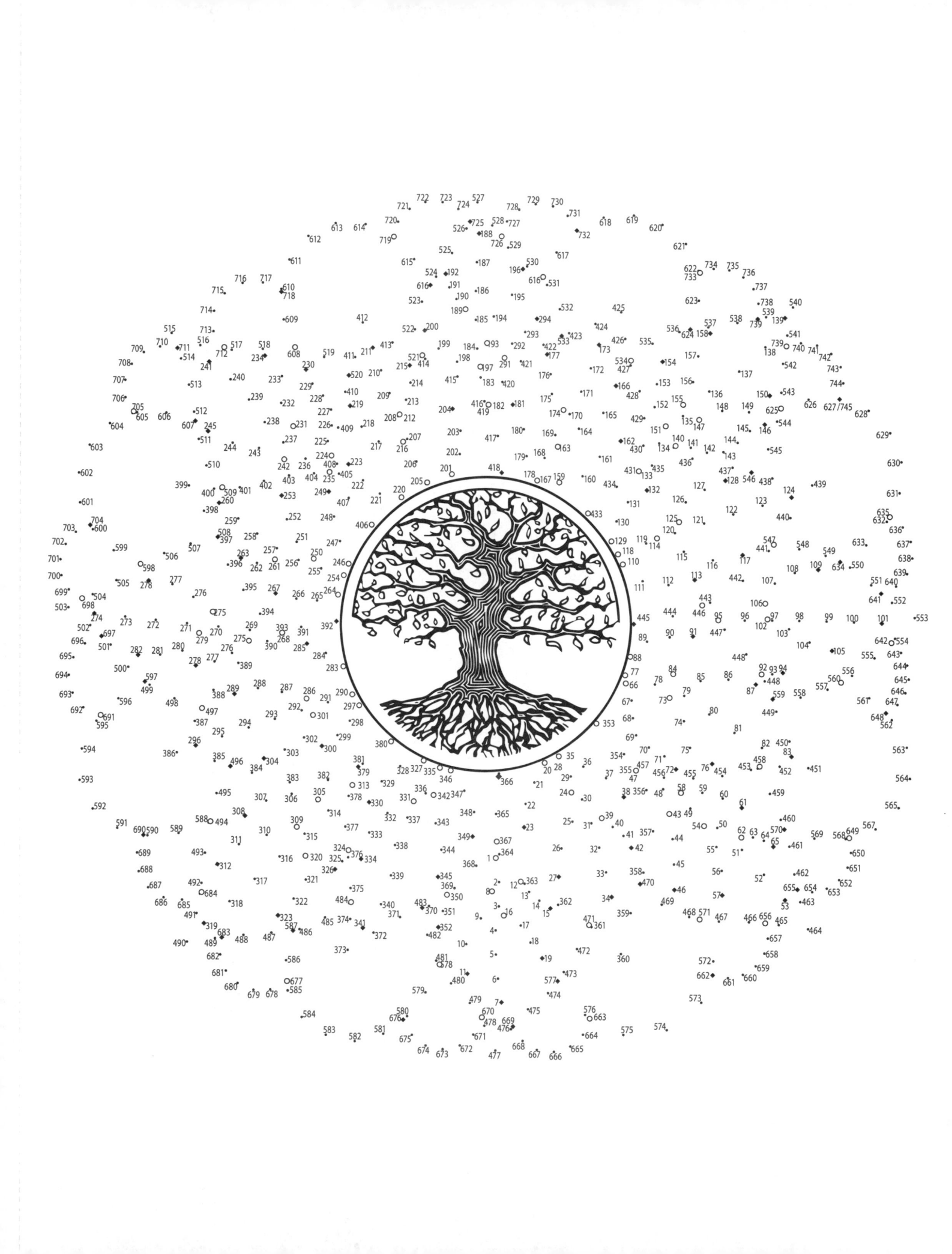

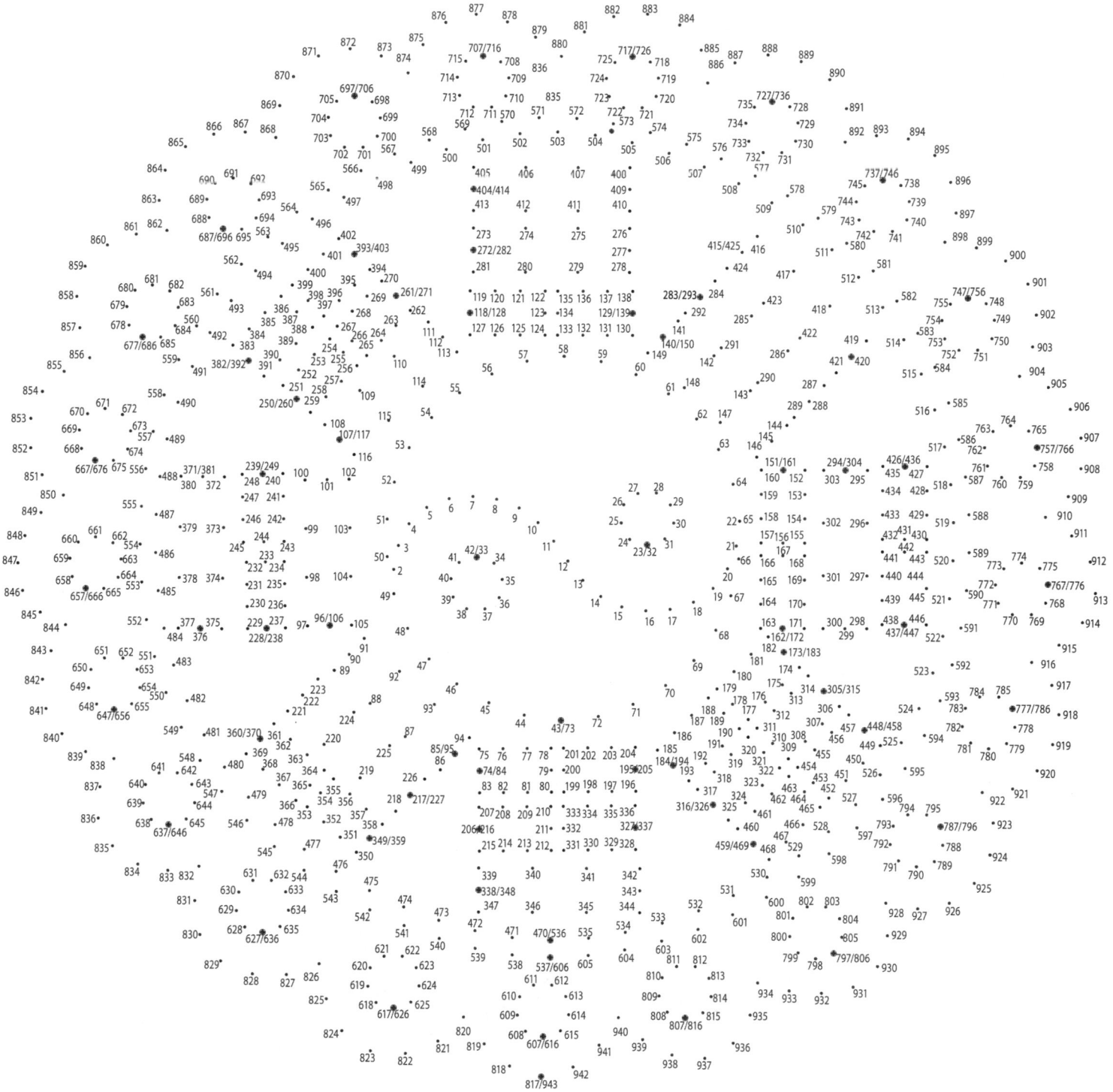

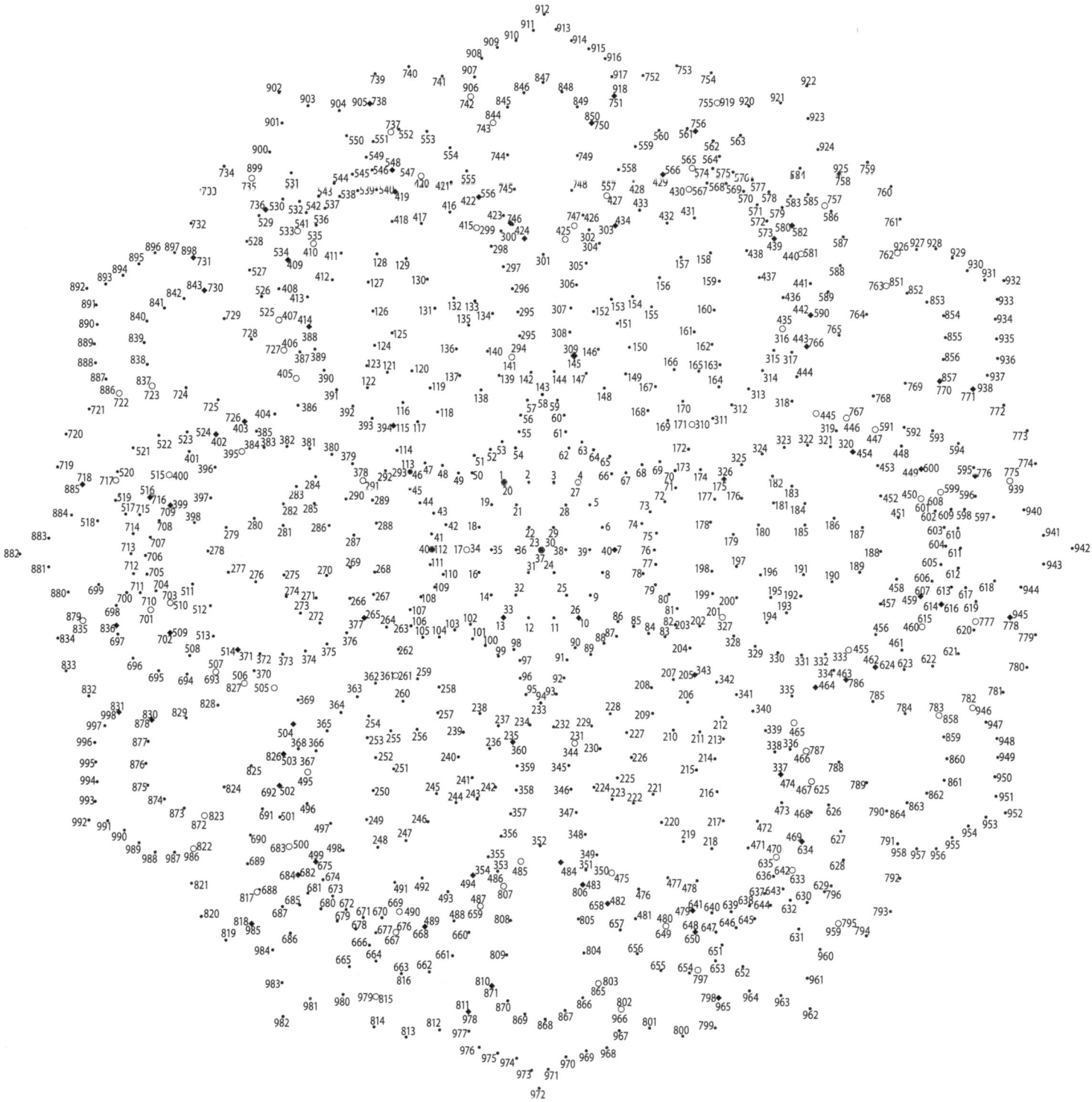

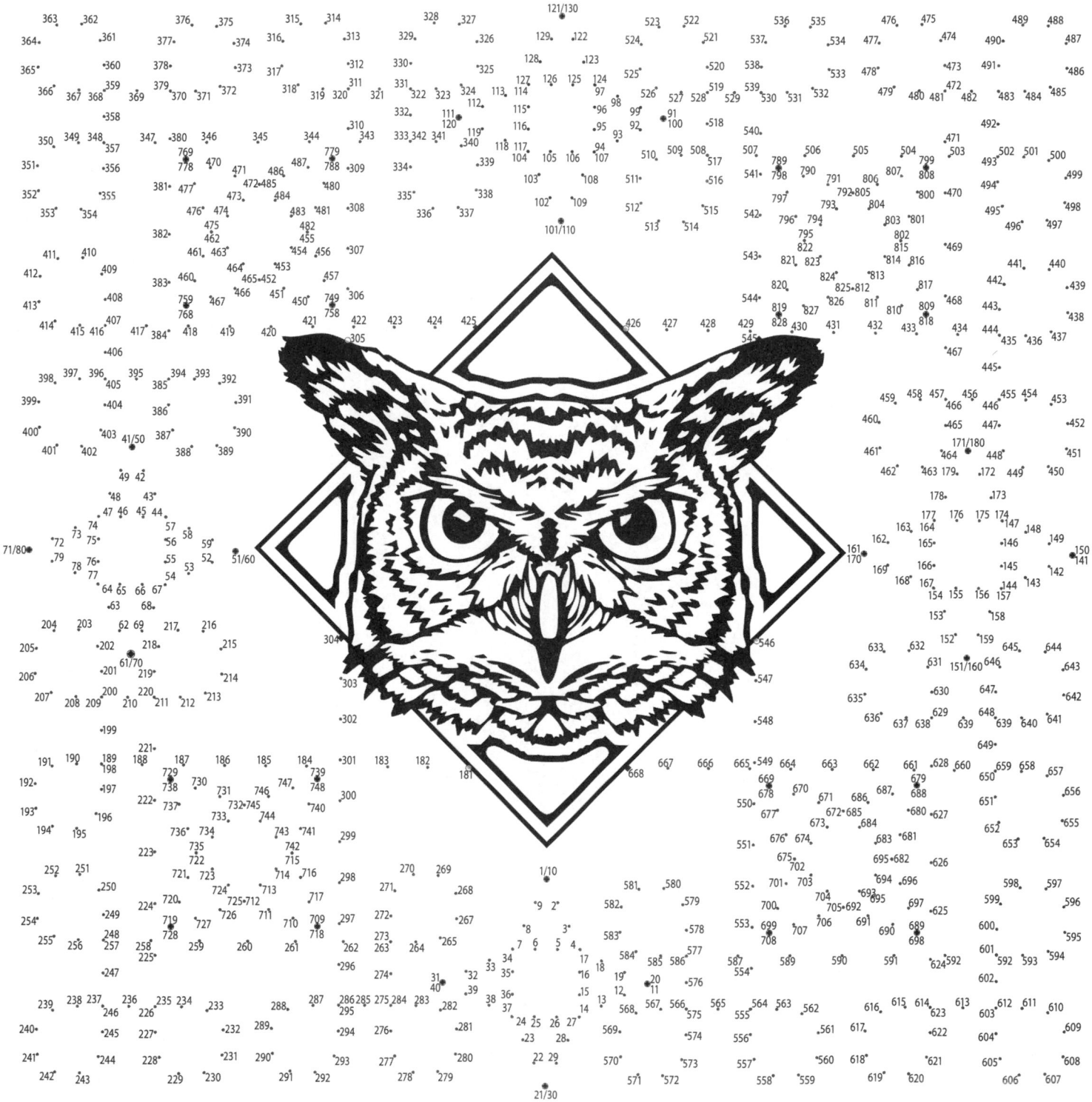

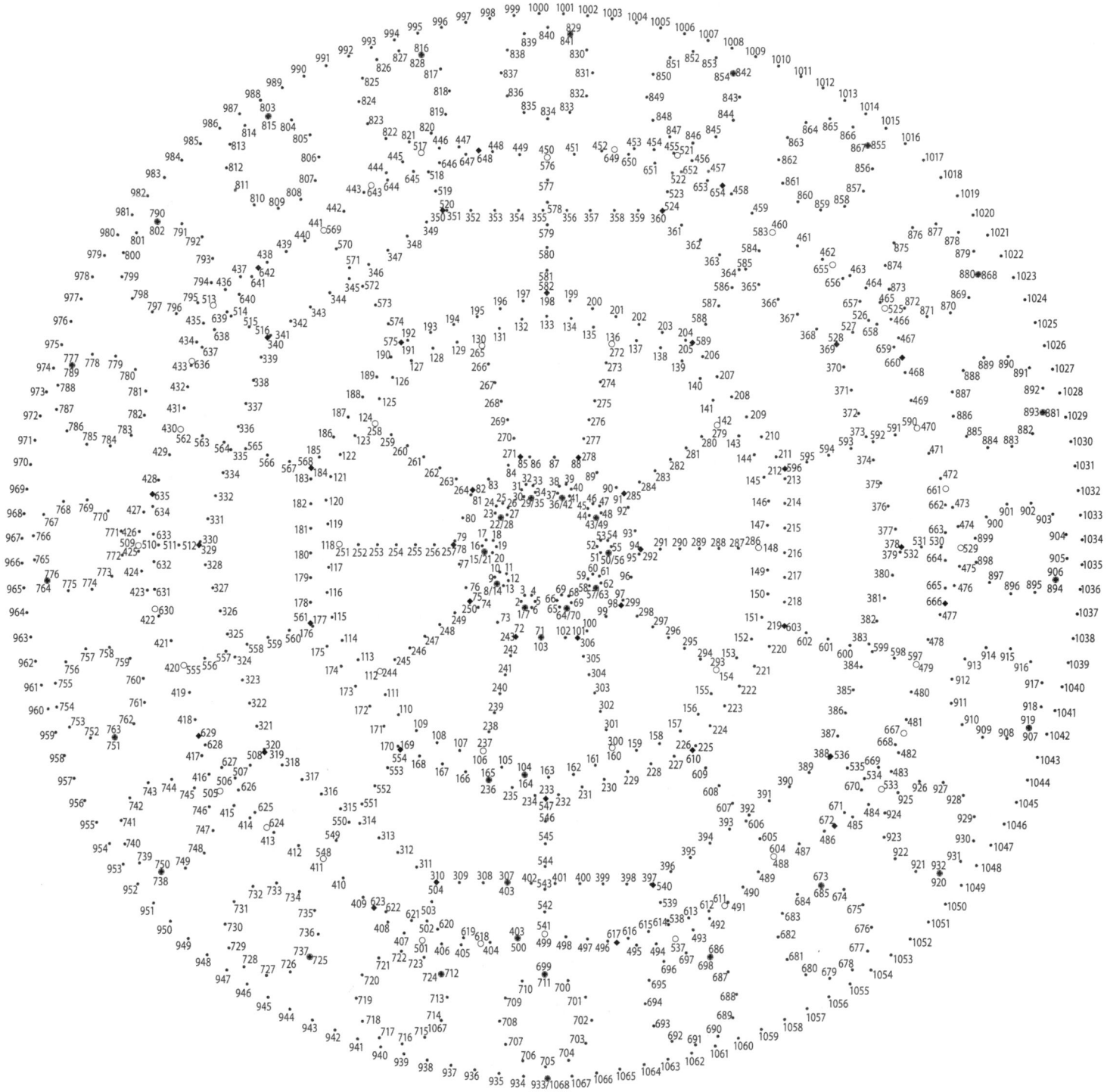

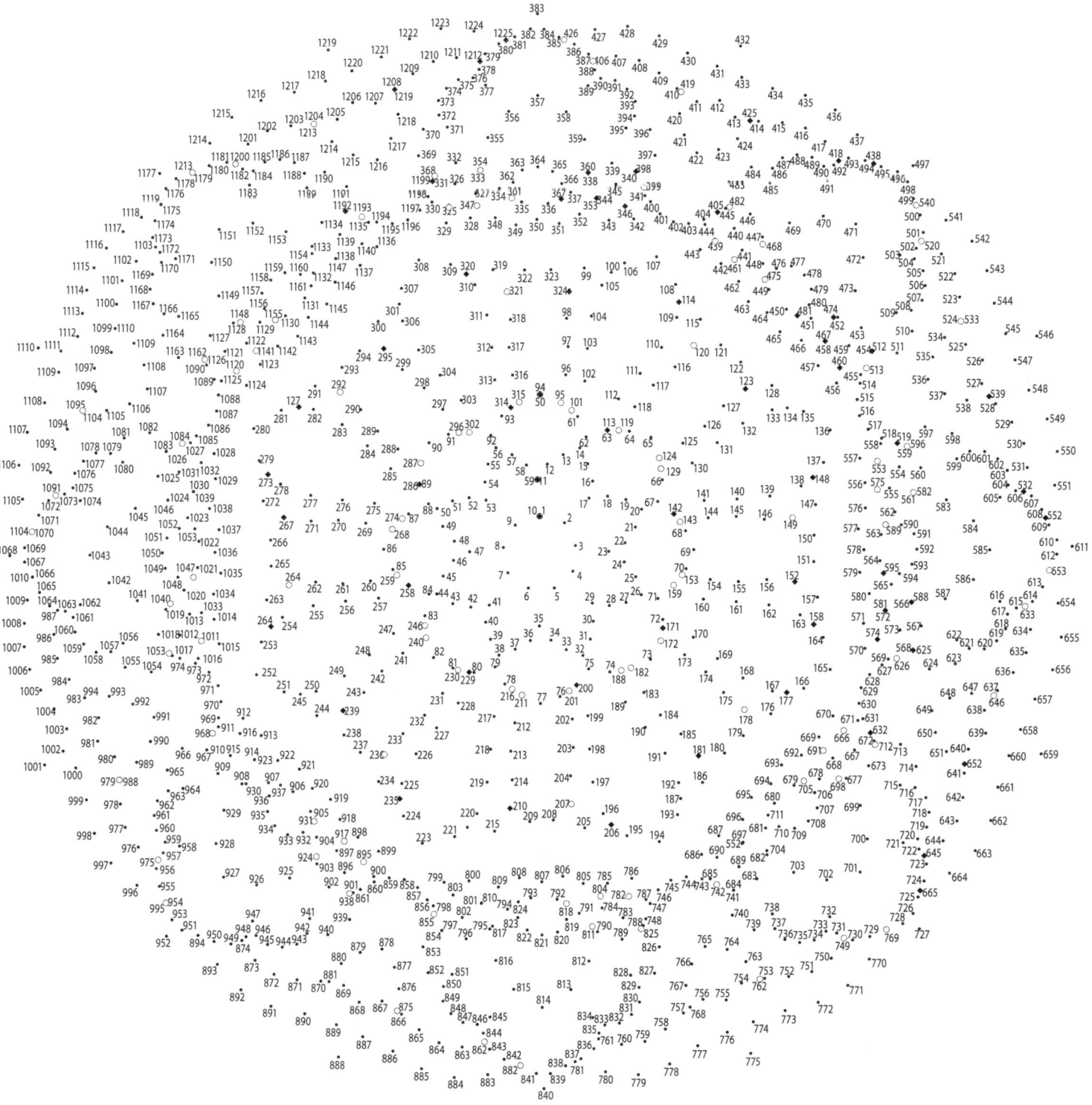

ANSWER KEY

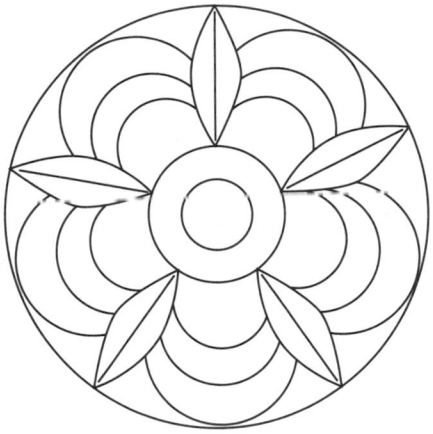

1

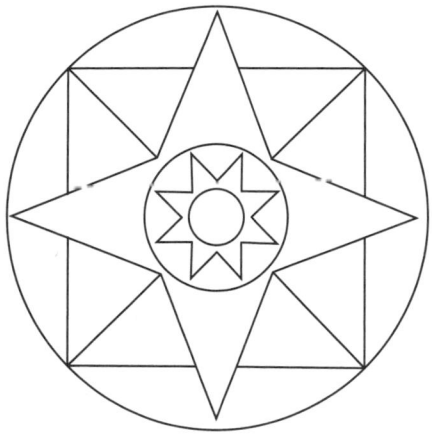

2

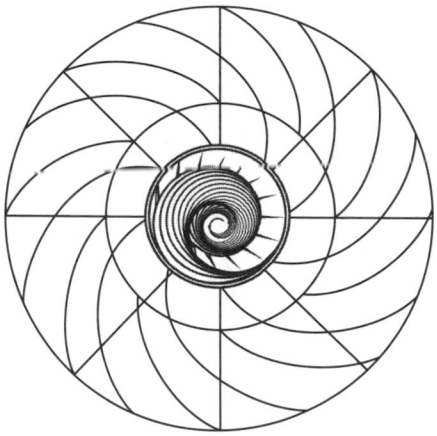

3

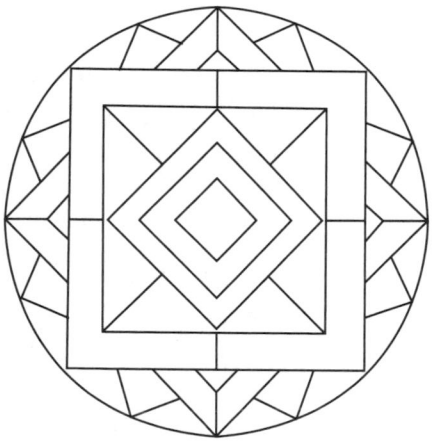

4

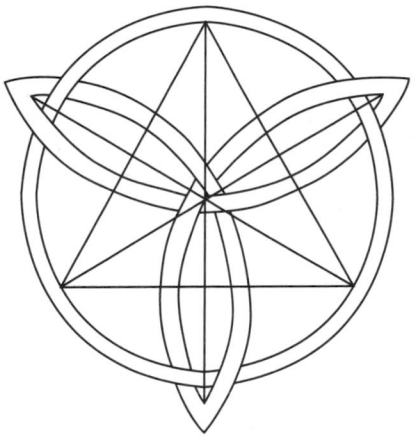

5

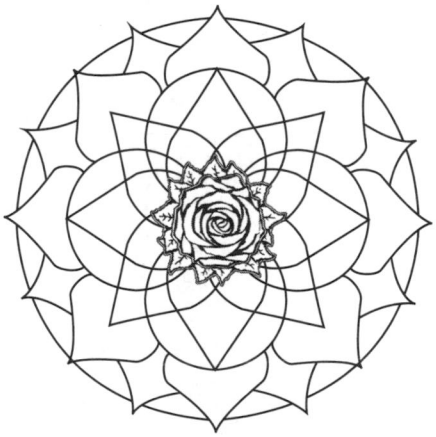

6

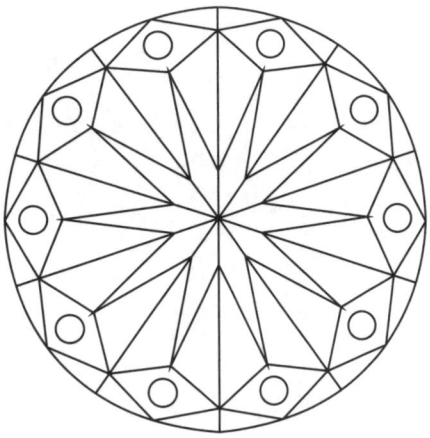

7

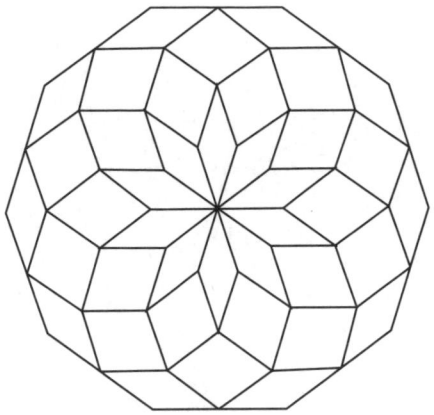

8

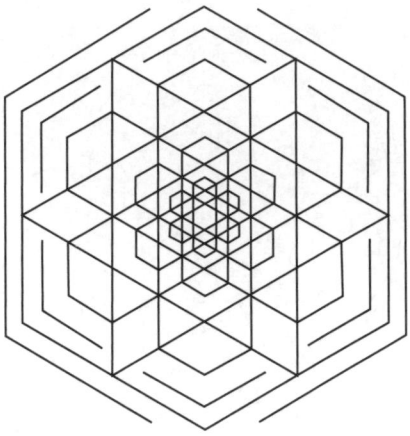

9

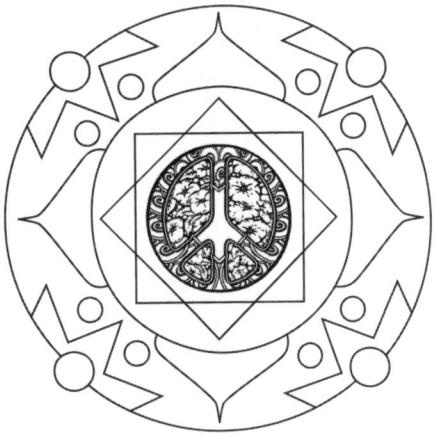

10

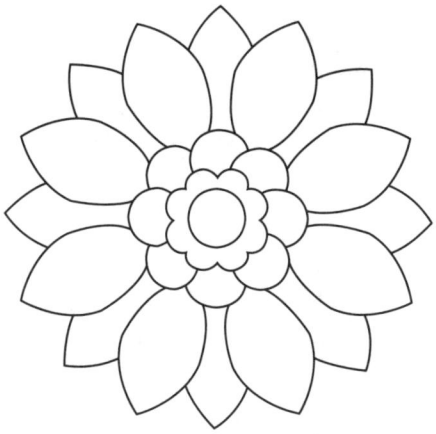

11

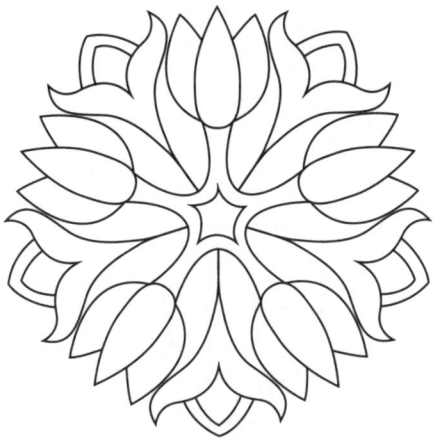

12

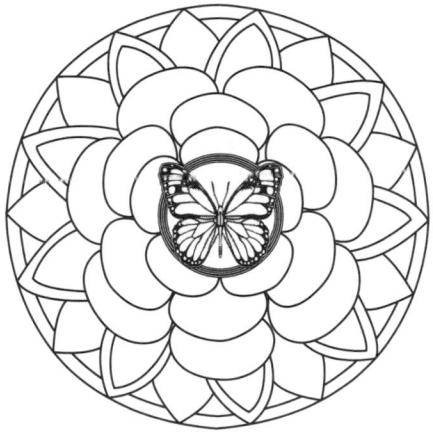

13

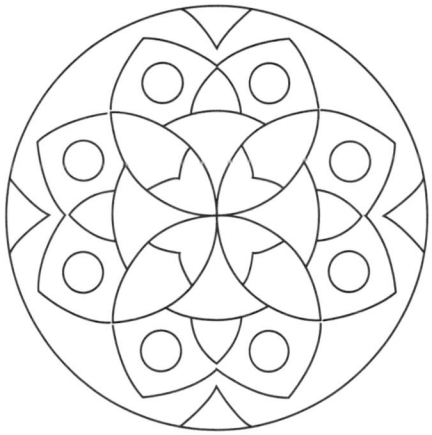

14

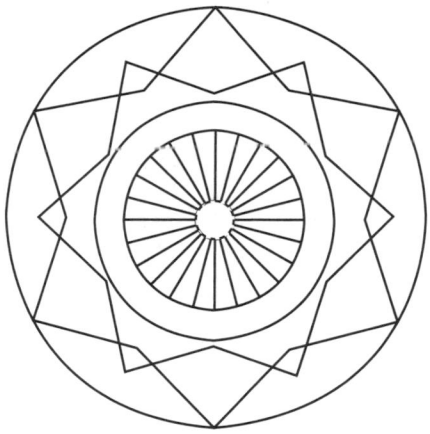

15

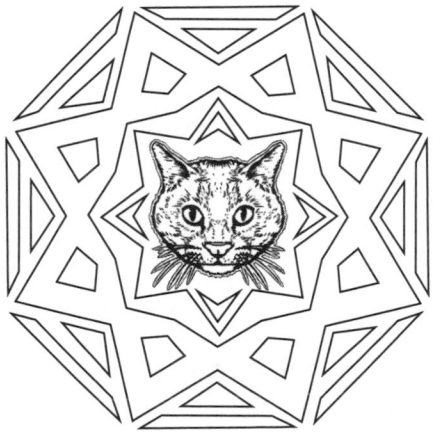

16

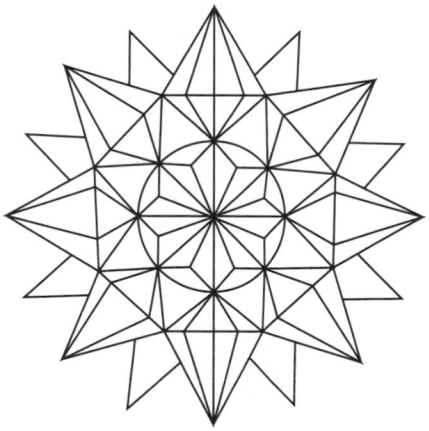

17

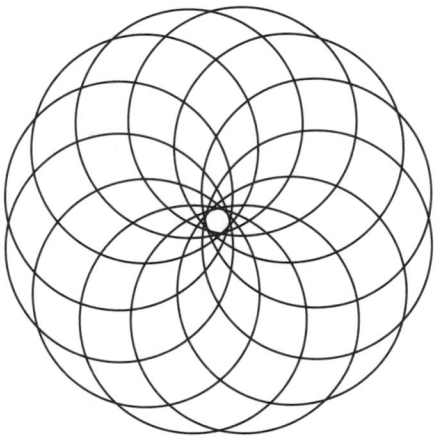

18

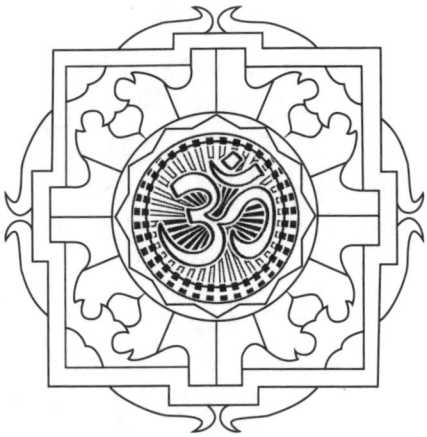

19

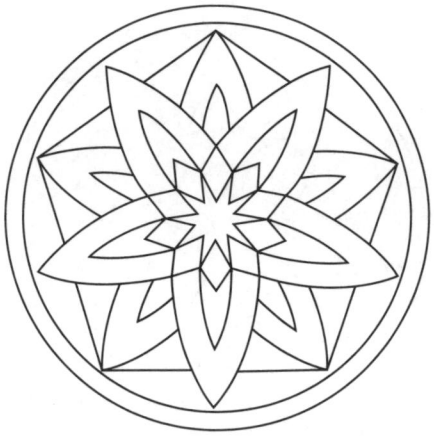

20

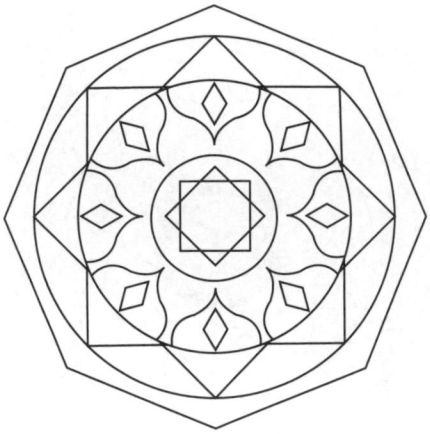

21

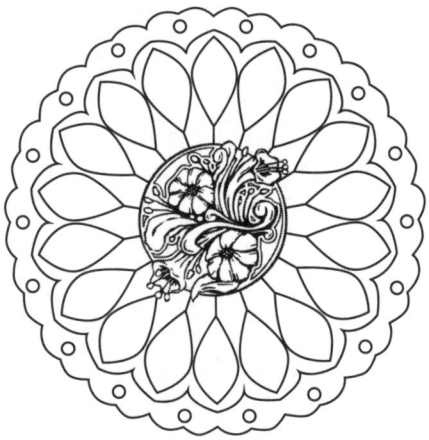

22

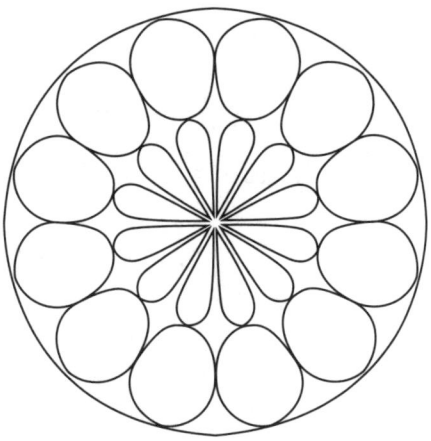

23

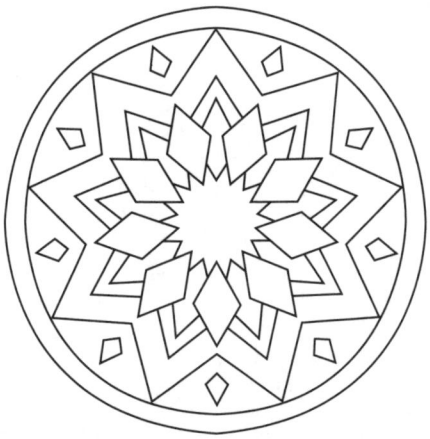

24

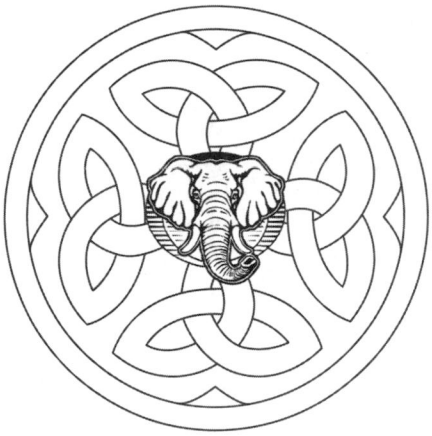

25

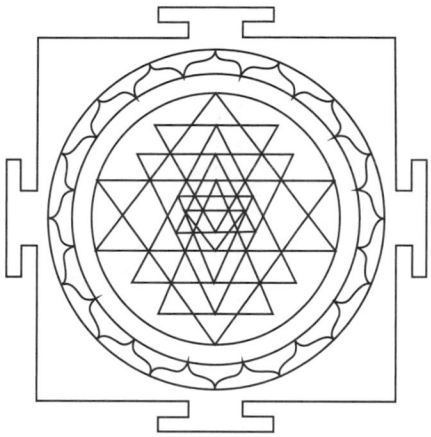

26

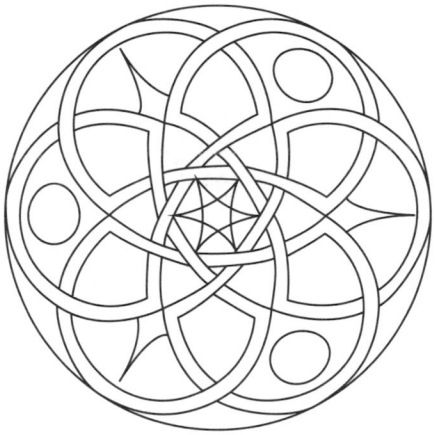

27

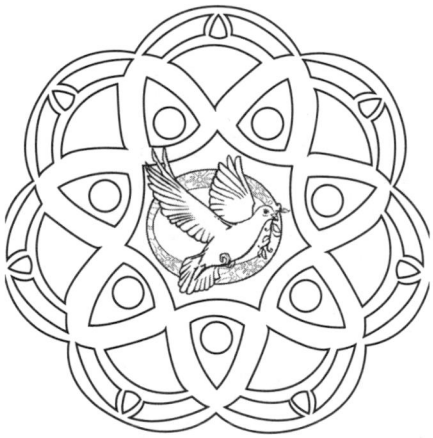

28

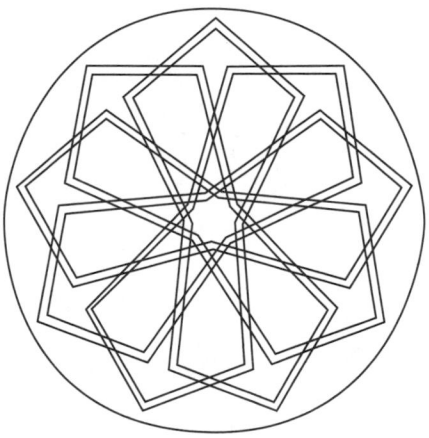

29

30

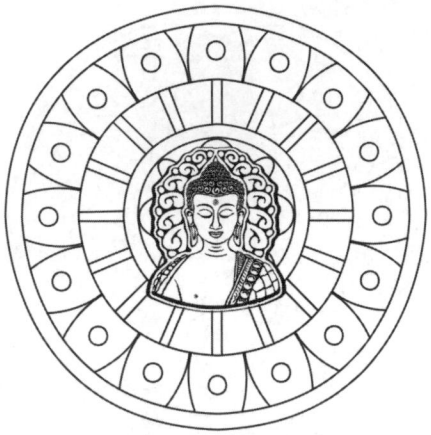

31

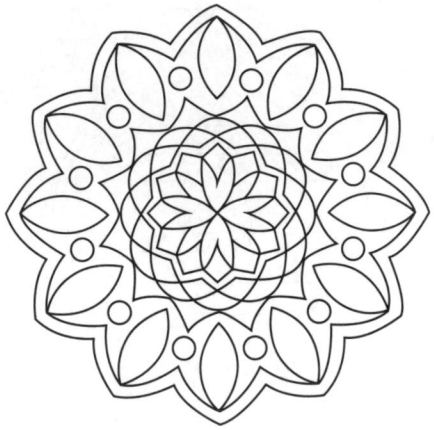

32

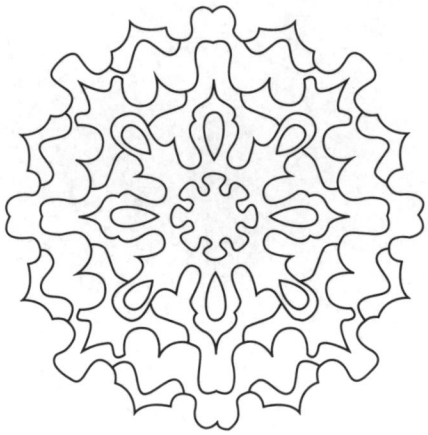

33

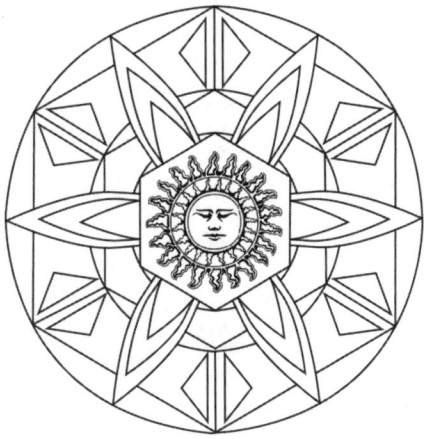

34

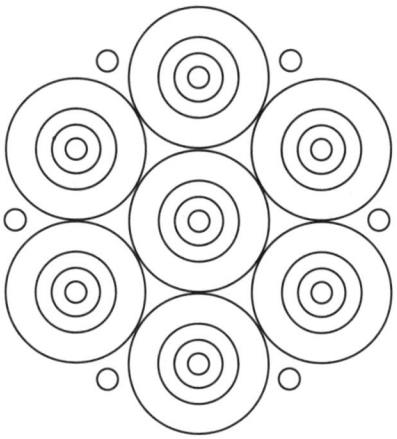

35

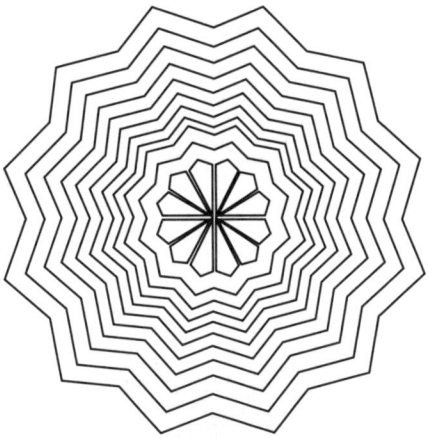

36

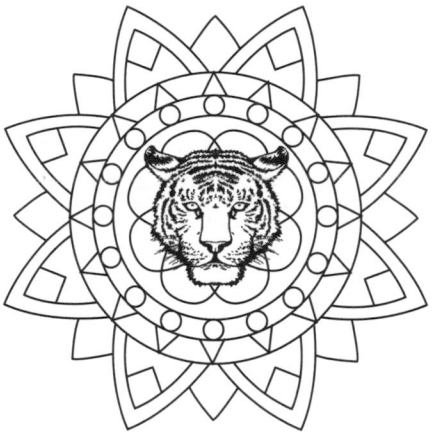

37

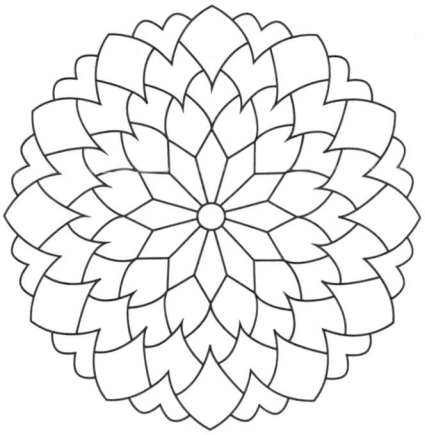

38

39

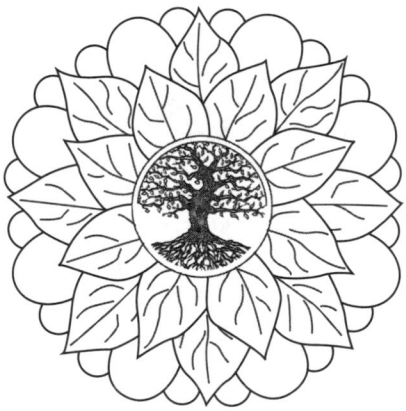

40

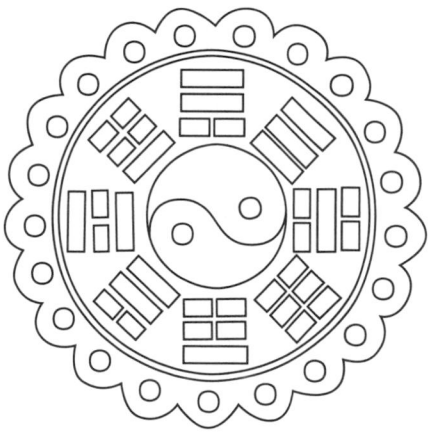

41

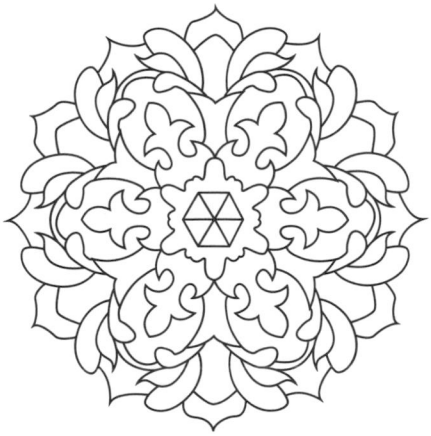

42

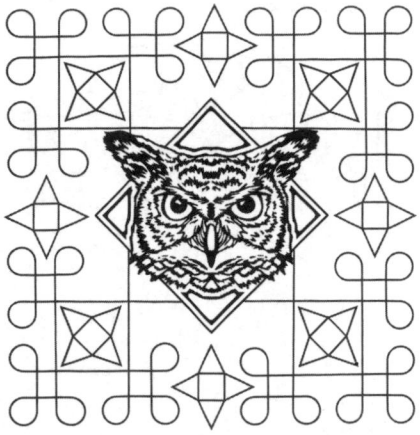

43

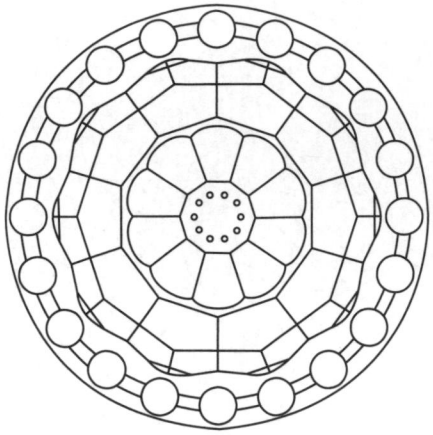

44

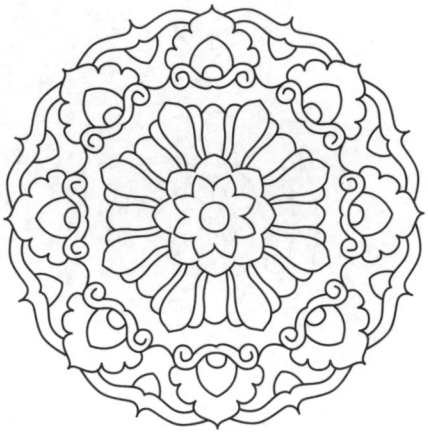

45